In the Shadow
OF THE
Almighty
GOD

DEDICATION

I dedicate this book to the power of faith, which has given me a greater understanding of our Creator. We receive grace through it to ride above temptations. As we grow spiritually, our focus is clearer and more firmed up on the destiny of God for our lives. By faith we receive the strength of God, and attain to the nature of Christ.
To God be the glory.

ACKOWLEDGEMENT

My acknowledgement goes to the Most Blessed Holy Spirit, Who through His team responded willingly to all the questions I raised in the writing of this book. Remain ever blessed in Jesus Name.

I acknowledge all the servants of God whose publications I am enriched by, which are merely an addition to the Word of God. To God be the glory.

TABLE OF CONTENTS

INTRODUCTION

The Word of God in Ps. 91:1-2 says, *"He who dwells in the secret place of the most High God, shall abide under the shadow of the Almighty. I will say of the Lord, He is my refuge and my fortress; my God, in Him will I trust."* This verse talks of El Shaddai, The Almighty God Who created all and is able to supply all needs. It also talks of dwelling in the secret place of this same God, that is, in His Will which is His Word; and as a result, abiding in His Shadow. This implies that the process of dwelling in His secret place comes before getting to His Shadow which is an upward spiritual movement.

There are different ways in which people can abide in His Shadow. The day you accept Jesus as your Lord and Saviour, get baptised and receive the gift of the Holy Spirit, you are already under His Shadow. There are those who will continue to abide in His Shadow because they are steadfast in their righteousness; while those who turn back to sinful life will find it difficult to continue to remain there. All genuinely repentant Christians will be forgiven and according to the Word, grafted back into His Shadow.

Abiding successfully in God's Shadow can only be made possible by the leading of the Holy Spirit. Ps. 23:3 says: *"He leads me in the paths of righteousness for His Names sake."* In order to dwell in His secret place as a believer, one has to strive to obey His commandments, that is, allowing the Word not the world or man to guide your decisions and impart its discipline in you. When one always praises Him, fellowships with Him, presents all problems and needs and that of others before Him, relies implicitly on Him through obedience, abiding in His Shadow will become a possibility.

There is an important lesson which the scriptures, especially Psalm 91 teaches about this. The promises of God are conditional to man's fulfilment of His commands. The psalmist in Ps. 91:2, tells us that because you have made the Lord your Refuge, your Fortress and your God in Whom you trust, He will protect you from the snares of the enemy and their pestilence. Within this context of protection, in verses 5 to 7 he states that, "You will not fear the terror of the night, nor the arrow that flies by day, nor the destruction that wastes at noonday." The benefits attached to its fulfilment is conditional to obeying the Word.

Verse 9 is conditional to verse 10, and states; "*Because you have made the Lord your Refuge, even the Most High your Habitation, there shall no evil befall you neither shall any plague come near your dwelling.*" Verse 14 states, "*Because he has set his love upon Me, I will deliver him. I will protect him because he knows My Name.*"
Ps. 24:3-4 asks; "*Who shall ascend into the hill of the Lord? And who shall stand in His Holy place? He who has clean hands and a pure heart, who has not lifted his soul unto evil, nor sworn deceitfully.*"

The Psalmist in Ch. 23 also talks about how Christ shepherds those who are in God's Shadow. He makes sure that they walk in safe places; that they are led in the paths of righteousness; that their souls are restored, and that in times of danger His Rod and Staff will always deliver them. Man has to learn to live according to the Will of God, and be totally submissive to His commands. One has to relate to God in righteousness, humility, reverence and fear. It is a two way agreement. Jesus obeyed God till death and as a result is now sitting at the right Hand of the Throne as promised Him.

When you are walking in the shadow of God you will be operating in His glory and according to John 17: 22, when one operates in His glory, the person will be living in divine love and according to the fruits of the Spirit. The life of Christ will be perceived in the way that person thinks, speaks and acts. The divine love of God, known as the bond of perfection, will be the platform on which the life of that believer has been woven. One comes to a realisation of his spiritual weakness, and relies on the leading of the Holy Spirit. God's condition has to be fulfilled before He can confidently accommodate one under His Shadow.

Walking under or abiding in His Shadow is not a prerogative of anybody or any particular group of individuals. All humans are creatures of GOD. His goodness in the form of the provision of sunshine, rain, air, water, food etc. are made available to all mankind. The Word of God is also made available to those who want to read and be guided by it. The blood of Jesus was shed to wash away the sins of all those who will believe and also receive Him. In the book of Acts 10: 34-35, Peter said, *"Of a truth, I perceive that God is no respecter of persons; but in every nation, he that feareth Him, and worketh righteousness, is accepted by Him."*

Obedience is as a result of faith and the fear of Him. This is the mystery of abiding in His Shadow and achieving salvation; that those living in darkness shall be given a chance to receive the Light of the gospel; and that Christ shall live in them through the Holy Spirit. As all continue to dwell in His Word and in His Love, they will draw others to His fold It was said in Rom 10:20; *"I was found by those who did not seek me I was made manifest unto them that asked not after me."* The gate of the kingdom was opened to us the Gentiles. Therefore let no one now say, my ancestors were this or that before I was born, and I have been like them and will remain that way. This Word is being made available everywhere today to inform and to transform minds into righteousness. Pray that God will forgive those past mistakes made in ignorance. The Will of God is that man should worship Him in righteousness, have faith in Jesus, and live in His divine love in His Shadow.

Through the process of sanctification by the Holy Spirit, man finds himself moving from an old sinful nature into righteousness, as his responsibility to offer to God a devoted heart, and to love others as himself becomes

11

clearer and is being fulfilled.

This book will explain at length the relevant steps necessary in order to abide in God's Shadow, especially at this crucial end time preceding the period of tribulation. These steps will be identified under the topics shown below. The book will conclude with a summary of facts explaining the positive and negative consequences of abiding in His Shadow. There are also very relevant prayers that will come in useful at this end time.

The topics that will be discussed will also provide answers to the following questions bugging the hearts of people at this end time.

Is man walking in the Shadow of God or that of the world system with its lusts and enticements? Ps. 91:1

Is man living in the spirit or in the flesh? Gal. 5:16

Is he aware that God still loves Him and is still waiting for him to repent and believe in the Lord Jesus Whom He sent to rescue all from sin? John 3:16.

Does man know better than God Who created and teaches him knowledge? Ps. 94:10, Ps.32:8

Has man come to the true realisation of who is currently

directing the worldly elements and regulating the lives of everyone in the world?

Is he aware of the current preparation in the spirit realm for the imminent arrival of Christ? John 14:3. Is he aware that Christ's coming will signal the beginning of judgement for man, and the process of the termination of the present heaven and earth; and the replacement by a new one? Does man know that in order to qualify for the new heaven and earth, one needs to be spiritually reborn? (John 3:5, 2 Cor.5:17) Are we spiritually reborn?

CURRENT POSITION WTH GOD

1 Jn 3:23 says, *"And this is His Commandment: that we should believe in the Name of His Son Jesus Christ, and love one another, as He gave us commandment."* If you and I will genuinely do this, we shall be able to fulfil the 10 commandments.

By relating to each other in the love of God, and exercising our faith in the Lord Jesus Christ our walk with the Lord will successfully lead to His Shadow.

An imagery of man's current positioning in the walk with the Lord can be likened to that of people climbing a spiritual tree that has a light shining at the top. This Light can be perceived as His Shadow. This is the Light referenced in the book of Jn 1:4 which reads, *"In Him was Life, and the Life was the Light of men."* This tree is almost covered by different groups of people at different spiritual stages in the climb towards His Shadow. Some who are climbing seriously are very close to the Light. They have decided to ignore all distractions against their movement upwards. They are happy, determined, consistent and almost getting to the Light to abide in His Shadow for ever. There are those who are midway to their destination. Some of them are contemplating giving up because it would appear as if the journey is not proving to be as easy as was expected. They had spent the greater part of their time complaining about the difficulties, suffering and oppositions they are encountering.

The Lord is seriously opposed to complaining. It is indicative of lack of faith in His ability to deliver. These ones are also constituting a hindrance and discouragement to the group directly below them who are zealously waiting to push upwards. They are standing on the Word of God in Deut 28:13 which says; *"The Lord will make you the head and not the tail; you shall tend upwards only and not downwards; if you obey the commandments of the Lord your God."* Those experiencing difficulties as Christians should try not to become sources of discouragement to others. There are also those who are still standing around the lower part of the tree. They are just hanging on as branches at the lower part of the trunk of the tree waiting for a miracle to propel them upwards. As they quote 1 Sam.2:9 which says; *"For by strength shall no man prevail."* They seem to have forgotten the scripture in James 2:14 which says that *".....faith without works is dead."* You need to be doing something to justify your faith; then the Holy Spirit will come to empower that action.

There are also those who are sitting at the bottom of the tree because they have not decided on the need to participate in the climbing. They are not knowledgeable about the requirements of the scriptures and are currently more distracted by the world, its snares and pleasures, as compared to the inconvenience and suffering involved in the climbing. They may be described as being born again in the flesh and not in the spirit.

This tree also represents what Christ stands for, and man's growth in the fruits of the Holy Spirit (Gal.5:22). The climbing also shows the gradual process of human sanctification by the Holy Spirit, based on the willingness, faith, love, and obedience of the climber in the Word of God. It can also be referred to as the climb towards Christlikeness. The tree can be perceived as the narrow way of holiness (Isa. 35:8). From a very far distance, the tree looks like a giant vine tree covered by branches with a lot of movements within and around it. Jesus said in Jn 15:5 *"I am the Vine, you are the branches. Those who abide in me, and I in them, bear much fruit, because without me, you can do nothing."* If you abide in Him, you are abiding in His Shadow.

For the group still sitting leisurely at the bottom of the tree, it is a question of the right timing to commence the walk with Christ. Some are waiting to secure a better job; others to set up family; some to get a mortgage; and there are those waiting for a financial breakthrough. As the waiting continues the set date for the judgement of man draws closer.

It is when one commences this climbing mystery on the tree by following the usual step of repentance, confession of sin, baptism and restitution; that the transformation from a sinful life to a Christ like life begins through the transforming power of the Holy Spirit and the Word. He is the One to position you in the Shadow of the Almighty.

THE BLOOD AND THE WORD

In order to abide in the Shadow of the Almighty one has to have the right relationship with Him. Our perception of the Lord, will determine our relationship with Him. If we perceive Him as the Son of God Who paid the ransom for the sins of man with His shed blood, and believe that there is no need to commit those sins anymore, we shall strive to relate with Him in obedience and dwell in His Shadow.

Our relationship with God is primarily based on the blood of Jesus and the Word. It does not matter what background you are coming from, or the sins you committed in ignorance and unbelief. The precious gift of repentance based on the blood of Jesus, changes everything. All believers are supposed to work out their sanctification by the Holy Spirit, in the way they live their lives; by living in the spirit not the flesh. Most of us who came from worldly backgrounds, and have committed all sorts of sins relative to such backgrounds before we believed have discovered the urgent need to begin to submit to the cleansing power of the blood and the Word. It may not be easy but that is the only way to edge out of sin. A divine voice ones said to me concerning dealing with sin, "Even if it has to kill you" (Heb.12:4). Another voice said over a different issue of disobedience, "Run for your life" Rom. 6:23.

As you feed the spirit through more knowledge and understanding of the Word of God, your mind gradually begins to release thoughts of righteousness, love, peace, fruitfulness, goodness, faith, joy, gratefulness etc. Negative thoughts gradually disappear under the guidance of the Holy Spirit.

Victory for the believer comes primarily through the blood (Rev. 12:11). As we partake of this blood and appropriate its cleansing power, we develop the characteristics and the attributes of Jesus, which are also that of God.

It is written in the book of Jn 6:53-54; *"Most assuredly I say to you, unless you eat the flesh of the Son of man and drink His blood, you have no life in you. Whoever eats my flesh and drinks my blood, has eternal life, and I will raise him up at the last day."* What Christ is saying is that if you drink His blood and eat His flesh through obedience and faith, that spiritually you are establishing a divine link to eternal life which is in Him. The blood and the flesh represent His divine nature. This is what the sacrament reminds us of.

To receive this grace, man has to prove to God that the cleansing power of the blood of His Son can be perceived in our faith and righteousness. We have to believe that it is possible to live a sinless life. Only in the practical demonstration of this belief can God be satisfied that we have accepted Jesus as a propitiation for our sins.

All Jesus is saying is, my blood has been shed for you so that through obedience, you can come and spend eternity with me in My Father's Kingdom. Let us work together, relate together in understanding and fellowship in the way we think, speak and act. Receive My Grace through obedience and faith, and the journey to the Kingdom will be easy as you yield to the leading of the Holy Spirit. Abiding in the Word of God is abiding in His Shadow. The Word is referred to as the Perfect Law of liberty. Scriptural liberty denotes freedom from the bondage of sin and its punishment. The Word is the Lord Himself telling us how to relate to Him and be like Him and avoid the second death.

Js 1:25 reads: *"But he who looks into the perfect Law of liberty, and continues in it, and is not a forgetful hearer, but a doer of the Word, this one will be blessed in what he does."* When we refresh ourselves with the Word of God on a daily bases, a healthy relationship between us and God will be established. These are the important questions to ask ourselves every day.

Have we read the Word sufficiently enough to understand it? Having read it have we opened our hearts for the entrance of the word by studying and meditating on it? Having allowed it to enter, did we allow it to dwell in us by practising and living our lives according to its requirements? What changes has it made in our hearts in terms of the way we now think? How like Jesus are we, with regards to His characteristics and attributes?

Jn 2:6 reads *"He who says he abides in Him ought himself also to walk just as He walked."* If you only hear or read the Word without meditating or thinking about it, you may not know how to apply it to the way you relate to the Lord and your fellow human beings. You will also not grow or be transformed in your mind. This is because you have not fully understood and sufficiently thought about it. The wisdom of the Word which is the wisdom of God, requires time. It is not what one can articulate at a glance or first reading. In order to get your bondages broken you have to allow the wheels of the Word to grind steadily, deeply and confidently at its own pace, because it is already programmed and settled in heaven. We shall all make it by the grace of God.

Under His Shadow, the Word of God provides us the hedge of His protection. The book of Eccl 10:8 says that whoever breaks the hedge, that is, disobeys the Word, the serpent will bite. That bite loosens your spiritual hold on God and invites suffering into your life.

We go wrong with the Word of God on which our relationship with God is based because we do not treat it as sacred. The Word is God Himself instructing us on how to relate to Him. Most people may have serious questions to answer because for fear of losing congregation they compromise the Word of God they preach. God is interested in having the right people in the church, and not a multitude where none is qualified for heaven. While in the spirit, I was in a church filled with many people. It used to be a few membership congregation. While there, a quiet voice said to my hearing, "all these are wrong people."

The Word is so powerful, authoritative and self-evaluating, that it immediately, and always recognises those who are serious with it, and those who are not. It can only be to you what you are to it. (Ps.18 : 25b-26).

FEAR AND REVERENCE; A REQUISITE FOR HIS SHADOW

God is Mighty and Awesome. His divinity, power, purity, and love and so on, incites holy fear and reverence. A relationship with Him based on fear and reverence has a chance of success and can guarantee a healthy stay in His Shadow.

Fear with caution can be as a result of the knowledge of the consequences of failure, and can induce obedience. It can also be based on the need to please God, which is based on a strong conviction of the truthfulness of the good news of salvation. It can also compel one to act cautiously in order to escape from the snares of the devil. Fear and reverence for God also instils discipline. The Lord is held in reverence as a role model, highly exalted. Ps. 89:7 reads; *"God is greatly to be feared in the assembly of the saints, around Him."* A holy fear of God becomes mandatory to His people. Acts 9:31 reads; *"And walking in the fear of the Lord, and in the comfort of the Holy Spirit, they were multiplied."* When your walk is based on the fear of the Lord, the Holy Spirit will lead you on a progressive walk and make you an achiever under His Shadow. Eccl. 12:13 reads, *"The end of the matter; all has been heard. Fear God and keep His Commandments; for that is the whole duty of everyone."* . Only the fear of God is justified

It is biblical to fear God and not man. Man instils fear through intimidation, lies and deceits. In the book of Matt. 10:28 Jesus stated that man should not fear those who kill the body but cannot kill the soul, but we should fear Him Who destroys both body and soul in hellfire. Misplaced fear gives rise to the scripture in Heb. 2:15 which talks of those who through fear of death, were all their life time subject to bondage to Satan.

It is written in Heb. 12:25 that we should serve God acceptably with reverence and godly fear. The fear of God is often referred to as a holy fear. This comes through love and the understanding of His Word.

His power, purity, love, faithfulness and knowledge, and the miracles signs and wonders He performs are more than sufficient to make man live in perpetual awe and fear of Him.

Ps. 2:11-12 reads; *"Serve the Lord with fear, and rejoice with trembling. Kiss the Son, lest He be angry, and you perish in the way, when His wrath is kindled but a little."* This is a favourite passage in the Bible. It is man's responsibility to live in holy fear and obedience to God. This will guarantee peace in His Shadow.

Man's greatest fear is of death. Heb. 2:15 testifies to this. God holds the key of death and hell in His hand. The defeat of Satan at the Cross of Calvary has destroyed the fear of the devil and death in the lives of believers, so that they can walk in the fear of God alone. The Word of God in 2 Tim.1: 7 states that, *"For God has not given us the spirit of fear; but of power and of love and of a sound mind."* This makes any act of unjustified fear a sin. May God have mercy on all of us in Jesus Name.

1Jn 4:18 reads: *"There is no fear in love; but perfect love casteth out fear; because fear hath torment. He that feareth is not made perfect in love."* This is a very powerful statement because the whole point of Salvation is faith in Jesus and love for God the Father and for man. The Word has already told us that he who does not have love does not have God. It can be said from this that he who has unjustified fear does not have God. Unjustified fear alone is the enemy of faith and love on which salvation is based. This is why Satan's primary objective is to instil fear in the heart of man at all costs. We should all continue to pray against the satanic spirit of unjustified fear.

There is something like justified fear based on the right caution. In Jn 11:53-54, when Jesus noticed that the Pharisees were determined to kill Him, being that the time was not ripe for that, He never walked openly in their midst again. In Matt. 4:5-6 when the devil asked Him to throw Himself down from the pinnacle of a temple so that the angels would rescue Him, He did not misuse His privilege as the Son of God.

The following men who truly feared and reverenced Him, dwelt securely under His Shadow. Daniel feared God than he feared being abandoned to lions to devour him. David feared and reverenced God, and as a result twice restrained himself from slaying Saul when he had the opportunity. 1 Sam 24:1-22 and 26:1-25. Shedrack, Meshach and Abednego feared God more than being cast into a burning flame of fire. Dan. 3:22-25.

ABIDING FAITH IN HIS SHADOW

Genuine faith in God can be likened to knowing Christ so well that obedience flows naturally. It is a sure access into the Shadow of the Almighty. A relationship with the Lord based on faith in Jesus operates on love and comes as a result of the knowledge and understanding of the Word of God (Rom.10:17).

The Power of Faith

Faith is productive and has a limitless capability for victory. This is why the Word of God in Eph. 6:16 says: *"With all these, take the shield of faith with which you will be able to quench all the flaming arrows of the evil one."* It is a powerful weapon of defence and victory. By faith we believe that as we pray, God will answer through miracles, signs, and wonders.

As we read the Word we believe that it will eventually transform us into the image of Christ. By faith we all believe and expect we will all rapture with Christ on His return. As we endure persecution without complaint we know that Christ will avenge and reward us.

By faith we are able to love each other and live according to the fruits of the Spirit.

We also believe that our weaknesses are perfected by His Strength.

I know somebody whom the enemy regarded as helpless, and he continuously bombarded the person with attacks day and night. But God was always there in His mercy to deliver. Whether the attacks were coming in the form of sudden surge of over a hundred spiritual warriors in the spirit realm heading directly to destroy; or as a fired arrow heading forward to land; or even a situation in which the spiritual enemies had captured, bound, and was hastening away in their boat to their camp of destruction; or another situation in which the person was physically trapped in a room already engulfed with fire, and the only way out was to leap through the flames; or even another situation where an irreplaceable organ had been so damaged that the matter was terminal and the Lord had to come and perform a creative operation, even when a sudden terminal upsurge of a strange epidemic waiting to wipe out, or where a lion like animal was released and charged towards the person menacingly with his mouth wide open hoping to devour instantaneously etc. In all these, Faith unlocked the door of mercy, and the Lord was always there at each specific occasion to miraculously manifest and prove His Word, and glorify Himself. It is very risky to attack anybody abiding in the Shadow of the Almighty. Ps.105:15 reads: *"Touch not my anointed, and do my prophets no harm."*

It is when the Lord is at work, that He will open your ears to hear the enemy complaining and asking, the question; *"But what of all those things we projected inside the body? What happened to them?* On one instance when poison was administered, it was still the Lord who physically delivered from sudden death, according to His Word in Mk 16:18, *"if they drink any deadly poison it shall not hurt them."* It was the Lord who opened the ears of the victim to hear one of them asking; "But we made twelve insertions. What happened to two?

On another occasion, a direct arrow was fired. All that the victim heard was a voice that said, "Just step aside." The victim's eyes were opened to see a black arrow heading towards him or her. The person quickly stepped aside. It came straight near, turned back and returned on its journey out of the house straight to the body of the sender to the glory of God. These are likely experiences under His Shadow.

Remaining under God's Shadow is conditional. The Israelites of old were removed from the Vine because of unbelief, and the Gentiles who believed were engrafted as branches Rom. 11:20-21. While in His Shadow, faith compels you to be obedient, consistent and determined. The spirit of victory is a legacy from Christ to the believers. The believer fights to win because of faith in God, and the assured victory from Christ. He has already won that victory at the Cross. This fact has conditioned the believer to a perpetual victory irrespective of how long the battle goes. Let faith prevail in all your battles and relationships. The Bible says that the believer falls seven times and gets up, while the enemy falls into calamity Prov. 24:16. Christian believers are required to fight persistently without giving up because help will always be sent when it is considered necessary.

In as much as one is supposed to pray in order to defend themselves it is necessary for all to try and strive never to return physical attack for attack, or slander for slander In

Matt. 5:38. Jesus condemned the practice of an eye for an eye, and a tooth for a tooth, because the new covenant operates on faith, which works by love. Place your faith in the ability of God to protect and to deliver.

It is faith that provides the incentive to develop a confident walk with the Lord, if you have to walk into His Shadow. It is only faith that will keep you thriving there in the service of God. Faith is fundamental to our Salvation.

Do you believe that Jesus destroyed sin and the second death at the Cross, yours inclusive? (Rom. 8:2). Your Faith is based on what you believe of Him. Do you believe that the Holy Spirit is able to empower your desire and determination to do what pleases God, and that that holiness He wants you to emulate will be rewarded? Do you believe that if you follow Him in obedience you can attain a state of grace and eternal life?

Righteousness is the foundation on which faith thrives. Hence it is said that faith is the shoe with which the walk on the righteousness of Christ will succeed. When God first spoke to Abraham he had faith, but His righteousness might not have been well grounded. Hence God came back ten years after and said to him, *"Walk before Me and be perfect.*" Abraham obeyed, and his righteousness immediately hastened Sarah's conception and made him the father of all nations.

What those who operate on faith focus on is not their problems, but the promises of the Word of God as they relate to those problems, and on His faithfulness. All true believers believe that God is perfectly able to overcome problems when it is presented to Him in faith and according to His Word.

Jesus said in 1 Jn 5:4, *"For whatever is born of God overcometh the world. And this is the victory that overcometh the world, even our faith."* Abiding in the Shadow of God and His Son Jesus Christ based on faith, is not only the key to salvation and eternal life but provides a foretaste of the Kingdom of God. It is worked out in love and obedience. It is the dynamic power that will compel you to undertake risks which otherwise you will not dare to. This is a well-known Biblical story about the faith of Caleb and Joshua. When Moses sent the Israelites to go and spy out the Promised Land, they came back and narrated very discouraging reports of fear and impending failure; which destroyed not only their faith but that of the others. Caleb and Joshua with their unshakable faith, declared that they saw differently.

They saw it from the point of view of the promises of God to them. They saw a land full of beautiful tempting things waiting to be over run, more especially since those people do not have the support of God. They perceived the promises of God on those problems highlighted by their brethren. They also perceived the power of God on the problems, and this also strengthened and encouraged them in their plans and determination. This stance on faith and its application, eventually won victories for them. " all good things come from God above, Who is the Father of Lights ," and never fails. one may as well always follow His perception of things.

Faith also is more about knowing, understanding, and articulating the attributes of Christ in our lives. As we grow more and more in the knowledge and application of His attributes and our faith grows as well, we are strengthened in our relationship with Him and fellow human beings.

In the Old Testament, faith was preached as a great necessity for Salvation. The scribes the Pharisees based their faith on a future Messiah they conceived and not on the righteousness of God which is based on faith in Christ. Faith is the only way to appropriate the benefits of Salvation. Self must give way to faith on

Christ's victory. The righteousness of faith which Abraham championed is to believe and follow God truthfully in all his ways. Success and eternal life comes as a result of where one's faith is based on. If it is based on Christ Jesus, when temptations comes the Shield of faith will act as a protection.

Where then has man based his hope on? Is it on man, worldly goods, the flesh, money, social attainment and world recognition? We are at the time of the beginning of sorrows for man according to Matt. 24:8: that will herald the overflowing and the abomination of desolation as prophesied by Daniel's Seventieth week in Dan. 9:24. What we are witnessing is the unfolding of God's provisional plan for the reclamation of this earth as fully explained in the book of Revelations. The way out is faith in Christ Jesus. Faith demands that we respond to any attack, slander or temptation with joy, patience and prayers before God, Who has the ability to deliver.

THE BEAUTY OF HOLINESS

The beauty of holiness is exemplified in the Shadow of the Almighty. There is a difference between being holy, and allowing the beauty of God's holiness to radiate from the heart. When a heart is saturated with the love of God, and can willingly go beyond the accepted level of holiness to do more than is normally expected, the beauty of holiness radiates. This is the matchless inner purity and beauty of the Lord, which the Church is supposed to emulate. It would appear as if only a few believers are striving by His grace to get to this level. Some quote Matt. 6:34 out of context by saying: *"Sufficient unto the day is the evil thereof."* Although we are all still struggling with righteousness, we are seriously expecting to make it. The psalmist said in Ps. 27:4, *"One thing have I desired of the Lord, that will I seek; that I may dwell in the house of the Lord, all the days of my life, to behold the beauty of the Lord, and to inquire in His Temple."* A sound knowledge and the understanding of the Word, will create a good awareness of the beauty of its holiness and the desire to achieve it.

Jesus said in Matt.11:29, *".... learn of Me for I am gentle and lowly in heart."* One needs this Heart of Christ to be able to operate in the beauty of holiness. Patience, persistence, and living sacrificially is required. A relationship based on holiness will thrive successfully, but the one based on the beauty of holiness will be a lot better, and may attract the attention of the Lord faster. It will also accelerate distinctively a rapid spiritual growth in His Shadow. It is a sign of spiritual maturity.

It will glorify God to heal the sick always and to bless His children. Sometimes it will appear as if He does not easily release these very blessings that will glorify Him. One begins to understand the high level of God's faithfulness to His high level of Holiness. There is nothing imperfect in the way He dispenses His power even at the cost of restraining His Glory. All His judgements are true and righteous altogether. Here we learn from Him. It is not self that dictates, but the Truth of the Word. This fact of depriving Himself of glory until all the necessary conditions are met radiates His beauty of holiness.

In Eph. 5:27, Jesus said, *"...that He might present her to Himself a glorious Church, not having any spot or wrinkles."* This is a Church where people give and not count the cost; which feeds its flocks and not themselves; which is always zealous and not lukewarm for the love of God; a church that is intolerant of evil; endures persecution joyfully and without complaint; which is always ready to win souls for Christ; where people fight for Christ and not heed the wound; where people toil for Christ and not seek for rest; where people humbly serve and not mind the shame; where people do not seek for self-recognition. Where leaders do not fear the loss of membership of financial supporters, at the risk of speaking the truth.

The beauty of holiness demands total separation from sin, in order to avoid the little leaven that leavens the rest. Abiding in His Shadow, is also about getting rid of that leaven that flaws human relationships. This demands that one focuses only on what is good about people, not on their faults. Awareness of own previous faults and mistakes, can give rise to a feeling of compassion and sympathy towards the criticised person, realising that the one being criticised is far better than him or her. Jesus advises that evil should be overcome by good.

Behaviours that Can Radiate the Beauty of Gods Holiness

1. When all hope is completely lost, and the spirit of despair and panic seems to rise. The beauty of holiness demands mountain top faith that enables the heart to continue to rejoice and sing the praises of God, knowing that God's Strength is made perfect in weakness.

2. When you are deeply hurt and you forgive and ask God to forgive those who hurt you, even like Stephen in Acts 7:60; although they have no plans to repent. When these same people urgently require your help on specific occasions and you continue to help because of Christ.

3. When you are really sick and you still go out to work for God as usual knowing that Jehovah Rapha can turn your situation around within a twinkle of an eye. Mk 9:23.

4. When somebody unlawfully takes what belongs to you and you do not go to fight to get it back. Mk 5: 38-41.

5. When you are very aware of the fact that the enemy is seriously and secretly trying to take your life, but you are still praying seriously to God to save the life of that enemy.

6. When you are always thanking God for the good and the bad in your life as in 1 Thess. 5:16 and attributing all blames to yourself.

7. When you are genuinely trying as much as is possible to live a controlled life especially in your feelings and emotions, and to deny the pleasures of sin and the flesh. 1 Cor. 7:9, Heb.11:25.

8. When you always allow the spirit to lead you by making your body a living sacrifice to God. Gal. 5:16. Honouring God with your body.

9. When you do not only attribute the glory to God when any good thing happens to you but also quickly dissociates yourself from consciously and unconsciously stealing His glory.

10. When you always love your enemies and bless those who hate you. Matt. 5:44.

11. When you are focused only on Jesus as your standard and not on man, and you allow all your decisions to

honour and glorify God. Heb. 12:2. Although Gods Will may always clash with yours and attract persecution and suffering, you continue to base your decisions on His will, knowing fully well that the Word of God says that a man shall not be tempted beyond what he is able to bear, but that God will always make a way of escape where there is no way. 1 Cor. 10:13.

12. When you always personally sympathise with the sins and weaknesses of others, knowing that there is none who has not sinned before.

13. When you identify particularly with the needs of the poor, the infirmed, sick, destitute, oppressed, widows and orphans etc. and often agonising in prayers on their behalf and to help whenever you can.

14. When one has ceased to be angry under serious provocation, or does not allow any anger to lead to sin.

It is through obedience to the Word and a totally broken spirit, that one can receive the grace and mercy that will radiate the beauty of holiness. We are all praying, and looking forward to attain this level of holiness in Jesus Name.

We must know that God is not a man that He will cast a doubt on the rightness of the exercise of His power and authority. His purity makes His judgements always pure and righteous; while His love makes them merciful. He will not do anything wrongly, and man will only get what He deserves.

Psalm 96:9 reads, *"O worship the Lord in the beauty of holiness."* Man's holiness is supposed to compliment God's perfect beauty.

It is His perfect beauty of holiness that is reflected in His creation. For the second time my eyes were opened to behold a group of his army suspended in the sky as in a carrier. They were heading towards the evangelical ground were I was standing with a pastor, waiting to start preaching. It was breathtaking to behold how their white outfit blended with their beautiful headgear and complexion. They radiated strength, confidence and peace. Ps. 96:6 says that *"strength and beauty are in His Sanctuary."*

THE WAY UP IS DOWN

The way to climb to the Shadow of the Almighty, is from the bottom line of sin. Every walk with the Lord starts from a position of unknown to the known. According to the psalmist in Psalm 86:11 all knowledge proceed from God. Man starts from his level of ignorance to learn knowledge from God. Ps.94 says that He created knowledge and is the One Who teaches man.

Every journey has a beginning and an end, and every step forward is supposed to be an improvement on the preceding one. The end is always expected to be better than the beginning, although sometimes this prediction may vary due to human error. Likewise there is usually a specified way to be followed in order to get to an expected end. In John 14:6, Jesus said, *"I am the Way, the Truth and the Life. No one comes to the Father except through Me."* The only way to access Heaven through God's Shadow is by developing the characteristics and attributes of Jesus which is also that of God. Jesus was born in a cold manger. He lay in a poor cradle sleeping, wrapped in poor clothing and the beasts in the stall lay about Him. His entrance into the world heralded the advent of the Spirit of humility, particularly to those who have the mind to understand and obey. In the book of Lk. 14:8-10 Jesus said that one should always sit in the lowest place and wait to be ushered to a high place, and not vice versa. In this humble position, you have only one way to move, and that is upwards.

If you have to go the scriptural way, go from pride to humility, from lack of the knowledge of God to the understanding and practicing of it, from disobedience to obedience, from selfishness to a state of divine love, from sin to righteousness, and from spiritual death to spiritual life. The way up has to be through the bottom.

This idea came into existence as a result of the fall of Adam and Eve, which instantaneously plunged man into a bottom line position of sinfulness. Sin will always plunge the sinner into this position. Since then, the struggle to rise from that bottom position assumed an established pattern in the life of man. Children from privileged or princely families still have to learn the rudiments of the position to be occupied and satisfy the required standards. Although the way up may be by inheritance, the heir still has to undergo training and be subject to the strict tutorship of teachers and guardians for many years until they qualify.

Man was without hope of eternal life, in total darkness, and doomed to destruction. The incarnation of Christ and His resurrection at last made available the only way of escape from the dilemma of sin. Isa. 53:5. Christ made Himself poor, of no worth, and a servant, so that man through His poverty may move up from this bottom position back to the original pure form in which Adam and Eve were created before the fall. Man can now advance upwards towards the nature of the Son of God, as one is gradually sanctified by the Holy Spirit, and the heart purified and transformed.

It is also known that Satan tries to resist every attempt of man to attain this position, but it is written that believers are more than conquerors through Christ

Who loves them and has already achieved victory for all at the Cross. (Jn 16:33, Rom. 8:37).

The bottom line is the satanic position, and man should not allow themselves to remain there for too long.One should focus on God's Shadow and eternal life. To climb out one has to develop the graces of faith and love in Christ Jesus, meekness and humility, obedience to the Word, discipline and especially, the fruits of the Holy Spirit. This involves giving up your rights and all the satanic demands of the flesh. This is a task which only the Holy Spirit can help you to achieve. If you do not start to lay a good foundation of this you may never be able to make it to His Shadow. The different areas from which one has to climb will be examined.

Climbing From Pride to Humility in His Shadow

The book of Lk.14:11 states that *"For whosoever exalteth himself shall be abased; and he that humbleth himself shall be exalted."*

Man is born ignorant, powerless, spiritually dead, into a world of false and degenerate moral values, satanic and manmade doctrines and vices that give rise to pride and self-glorification. It would appear as if the spiritual pollution is more than the physical. To God be the glory Who has provided a way of escape through Christ His Son.

Learning through the right and humble way, is likened to following the ways of a child. Jesus said, *"Except ye be converted, and be like a child, ye shall by no means enter the kingdom"* Matt.18:2. A child is humble minded, joyful, sinless, selfless and very unassuming, dependent, willing and eager to learn, obedient and trusting. A child asks a lot of questions with a desire to learn.

Matt.11:29 reads; *"Learn of Me for I am meek and gentle."* The emphasis here is on man's willingness to be led and to learn, and the subject matter to be learnt is meekness and gentleness. Humility is the fastest way to His Shadow and the Kingdom because it automatically gets rid of a lot of sins. It unlocks the gate of mercy in God's Heart. It subdues the pride in man so that he can believe, reverence and obey God and serve fellow human beings without self-consciousness. Without humility, the believer cannot be lead successfully to the Shadow of Christ.

In Matt. 3:15, Jesus said to John the Baptist, who was

reluctant to baptise Him, *"Permit it to be so, for thus it is fitting for us to fulfil all righteousness."* He had to humble himself before John in order to be baptised by Him. This fact emphasis the point that the way to make it upwards to the Kingdom is through humility, meekness, forbearance, self-denial. This is a state of complete brokenness. It is a powerful weapon of spiritual progress which should be woven in the whole fabric of the life of a believer.

In Isa. 66:2 God said; *"For all those things, hath My Hand made, and all those things have been, saith the Lord; but to this man will I look, even to him that is poor and of a contrite spirit, and trembles at My Word."* God wants to dwell through His Spirit inside the one who truly has a humble and contrite heart. The one who is completely broken. This is the one who appreciates the fact that he needs to improve his low spiritual nature. It is this type of heart that makes it possible for one to love others the way they love themselves, and to serve without feeling inferior.

The book of Rom. 15:3 says: *"For even Christ pleased not Himself; but as it is written, the reproaches of them that reproached thee fell on me."* At this stage, you have undertaken the responsibility to suffer for others. It is the highest level of humility known as brokenness. Flesh has gone, and people are beginning to think that maybe all is not quite well with you because you are totally insensitive to their attacks and derision and even pleasure.

Humility breaks all negative bondages, destroys satanic strongholds and partitions. It can be perceived as the righteous sacrifice for peace and reconciliation. This idea of rising from the bottom line helps one to build a foundation that is sustainable and able to withstand all temptations so that there will be no back crashing later in the Christian life.

Climbing through Hard work

You work hard to get to the Shadow of the Almighty, and you work even harder to maintain your position there, so that you will not be taken away. Hard work builds a solid foundation for success. This idea is operative in the world system by the law of demand and supply. Those demanding the services need to release enough money to pay for their requisitions. Those producing or rendering those services need to work hard in order to satisfy the standard of demand required of them and beat any competition. In the scriptural world, Prov. 28:19 reads:

"He who tills his land, will have plenty of bread to eat, but he who follows frivolity, will have poverty enough." One has to work hard in order to meet scriptural demands. Extremely hard work is needed in order to ensure a successful Ministry. The legacy of hard work which Christ left for man can be seen in Jn 5:17 which reads: *"My Father has been working, and I have been working."*

As a believer, if you expect God to bless you without working hard, be reminded that there are many unbelievers who are working extremely hard, and the Bible says that a labourer is worthy of his own pay. The law of seed faith and harvest which scripturally is the law of financial prosperity, has to be fulfilled (Gal 6:7-8).

Some relevant questions for the believer includes the following:
• Are you doing the right work that does not negate Christian values especially church attendance?
• Does your work lead people into temptation?
• Do you work in an organisation that endangers people's safety and health?
• Do you work in an anti-Christian organisation?

The Scriptural Pattern of Rising from Poverty to

Prosperity

You have to honour God with your work. Deut. 8:18 reads; *"You must remember the Lord your God for it is He that gives you power to get wealth, so that He can fulfil the covenant which He swore unto our forefathers, Abraham, and his seed even till this day."* Your blessing as a believer flows from that promise which God made to Abraham and his seed for ever. He promised, *"In blessing I will bless you, in multiplying I will multiply you."* This means that one will have to fulfil the laws of prosperity in order to be blessed. Always ask God to give you the determination to work hard.

• Js 1:17 reads: *"Every good gift and every perfect gift is from above, and cometh down from the Father of Lights, with Whom there is no variableness, neither Shadow of turning."* The only way to rise to receive this blessing is through obedience to the Word. According to 3 John 1:2 one has to grow in the knowledge and application of the Word before these blessings come.

• Is. 48:17 reads: *"I am the Lord your God, Who teaches you to profit. Who leads you by the way you should go."* He is the Restorer of that which is lost; and that way is from the downward position upwards through faith and obedience. The satanic way is to go from the top position downwards, because the evil one is a destroyer.

The Path of Seed Faith

• Lk 6:38 states the law of divine reciprocity; what and how you give will determine what you will receive from God.

• Gen. 8:22 states that it is God Who established that seed faith should lead to harvest.

• These scriptures teach the need to sow, without which one can hardly receive an increase. At creation, God gave man the power to live, grow and multiply. People are supposed to sow in the area of their needs.

• The general law of Divine reciprocity teaches that as you give or sow rightly, the seed will disappear and God will give life to it, and return it to you in a bigger and better form. You will advance from a level of poverty to that of prosperity as the time goes on. If you did not plant, you cannot harvest what does not exist.

• If you are expecting miracles from God it is advisable to deposit something worthwhile into His Kingdom. When you work for God, you are investing your resources. Time and concentration is also part of it. When you praise and worship Him you are sowing a good seed. When you work hard consistently in your academics or job, it is a good seed and you will attain a high standard of performance. You can sow in your moral life by allowing it always to conform to scriptural standards.

Jn 12:24 reads: *"Except a grain of wheat falls down and dies, it abides by itself; but if it dies it produces much fruit."* Jesus sowed His life for man's salvation. He opted to die on the cross in order to be glorified and to produce many righteous like Himself. It took Him years of preparation, hard work and denial, discipline, determination and obedience to God. This is the foundation of seed faith and hard work that bears good fruits.

The Spiritual Ascent

The Scripture makes us to understand that a body without the spirit is dead and that as sin kills the spiritual life of man so does salvation restore it. This fact establishes the need for one to be saved and operate in the spirit. One is born again in the spirit not in the flesh. When you accept Jesus as Lord and Saviour Christ Who justifies you removes the sin in you, and imparts the Holy Spirit inside to indwell you. He will guide, instruct, cleanse, and make it possible for you to eventually, walk away from future sins. He will guide you into the Shadow of the Almighty. If one has to walk in the footsteps of the Lord, it has to be done in obedience to the Holy Spirit, He is a special gift from God, to baptised believers to help them continue in the work which Christ started. Through sanctification, a gradual process of cleansing from sin to righteousness, the Holy Spirit creates in man a regenerated pure heart. This will make it possible for Him to worship God in love and righteousness. This is the whole point of salvation.

The Holy Spirit imparts His fruits in man so that he can live according to them, and consider them as the visible stepping stones on which to walk in Christ. He also gives man the power to challenge, combat and defeat sin. However, when one fails to live up to the fruits of the Spirit, He cannot guarantee that sin will not return to that person. There then lies the need for discipline, determination and perseverance in the lives of believers. The Word of God says in 2 Cor.3:17 that where the Spirit of the Lord is, there is liberty. This is liberty from sin and condemnation, because the person is no longer under the law, but under grace.

One has to guide against many spirits of the antichrist masquerading as the Spirit of God the Father and the Son. In the book of 1 Jn 4:2-3 we are given the necessary questions to ask them and also how to check out on what they say. Everything the devil says is to hinder the Will

God in His Word. Watch out for the spirit of control because the devil tries to dominate and to control. Every believer should strive to walk in the Spirit. The Spirit is the Spirit of Truth. Therefore walk in the fruits of the Spirit.

In Jn 10:11, Jesus says, *"I am the good Shepherd...My sheep hear my voice."* These are believers who operate in the Spirit; for the things of God are spiritually discerned. This requires spiritual awareness, and the understanding of the Word.

The flesh is man's carnal nature through which he is sold to sin. It is a satanic weapon that lures man away from the Word of God which is spirit and life. You cannot live according to the flesh, and grow in the spirit. The bad tree cannot yield good fruit. For the spirit to grow in man the flesh has to be crucified. Man should pray fervently for the power to successfully resist the satanic demands of the flesh, so that the Holy Spirit can take control; to maintain a clean vessel so that He can indwell and guide one upwards spiritually.

One of the most effective way to grow spiritually, is by living a humble and servant like life; having love for others and being obedient to the Word of God. This is a life of restraint and self-denial. It is necessary to cultivate a habit of accepting criticisms, corrections and being open to change no matter how highly placed or learned in the Word one is.

Spiritual growth also comes through the understanding and application of the knowledge of the Word of God and constantly waiting on the Lord. Through the sanctification of the Holy Spirit, the old habits of doing things will begin to disappear, and the new Christlike life will take over. The change may not be easy, given how far one has gone in the old habits. But with faith in the finished work at the Cross, as one's sanctification is worked out in the way that one thinks, speaks and lives or deals with fellow human beings, the flesh will be on its way out in Jesus Name.

When the lust in the flesh responds negatively to the enticement in the world, sin enters and gives rise to spiritual death in the life of the individual. This has to depart at all costs. What I was told spiritually, was that there shall not be found in me any flesh. If you are not growing spiritually, it means that your walk with the Lord and your relationship with him is also not advancing but deteriorating. We need to follow Him to grow spiritually (Rom. 8:9). This fact underlies the need for man to continue to respond positively to the sanctification of the Holy Spirit. Man's spiritual training and growth only ends when he gets to heaven. The devil's intention is to worsen any ugly situation that one finds himself in.

There were a lot of things which even His disciples needed an explanation before they could understand. Matt. 16:21-26. In Jn 6:53, Jesus said that except one eats His flesh and drinks His blood, the person would not have eternal life. Some disciples began to leave Him because they could only understand the literary interpretation of what He said. They could not discern its spiritual meaning and had no patience to wait for an explanation.

Peter had a vision in Acts 10:9-16 of a big sheet being let down from above that contains different animals, birds and reptiles. The Lord asked him to kill and eat. He had to reply that he had never eaten anything unclean in his life before. This happened three times. It takes spiritual discernment alertness, and understanding of the Word in order to catch up with the Lord's level in His understanding. This is why He gave believers the Holy

Spirit to keep them on course with his Will.

Scriptural Examples

The Rich Young Man. Mk.17:19. Jesus spoke to the young man who got up the ladder of prosperity in Mk. 17:24, and said; *"One thing you lack. Go your way, sell whatever you have and give to the poor. You will have treasure in heaven. Come, take up your cross and follow me."* The selling of those things will create a void in his life that may lead to emotional and physical torment. Jesus said that he should take the suffering and follow him because Jesus has something far better than his losses. Phil.3:8.

This issue of switching from worldly wealth to the spiritual has always been a major problem to man. The young man refused to build a new foundation on Jesus. He had climbed up the wrong way and as a result worships his money, which is idolatry. His foundation was laid on the righteousness of the law, not on faith and love in the Lord Jesus. Jesus is perfectly able to replace them, and also triumphantly lead him to heaven.

The righteousness of faith is: "Take up your cross and follow me." In order words forget the low estate and the inconveniences attached to it, learn and follow my ways in faith, and your gain will far surpass anything you can imagine. If the young man had acted according to what is written in Matt. 6:33 before acquiring his wealth, he might not have been asked to go and sell his goods. But in the circumstances of Matt. 6:24 which states that you cannot serve two masters, as his wealth would constitute a major hindrance to his concentration on the things of God, he was asked to dispose of them. Lust for wealth is not only covetous, but idolatry. It is after you have given your life to Christ, and are living righteously, that the Holy Spirit will empower you to get wealth, because you will be able to resist its distractions from the things of God.(Deut.8:18.).

Abraham, David, Moses, Joseph, etc. all came up from the bottom position. The disciples of Jesus had to relearn fishing. This time they had to fish for men. Paul the apostle, a highly learned lawyer lost all that he had acquired willingly, in order to learn of Jesus and work for Him. In Phil.3:7, he said, *"But what things were given to me these I have counted loss for Christ."*

Judah

He came a long way from the pinnacle of pride to the root of humility and love. When he and his brothers sold off Joseph out of envy and for the money they could get, they were only interested in themselves, and not in the agony they would be passing their father through. When they came to Egypt to buy food he had learnt to honour their father and to show love for others. Judah was prepared to be held a prisoner so that Benjamin would be returned alive to their father. The entire traumatic experience of discovering who Joseph was, and the hand of forgiveness kindness and love he extended to them instead of hostility, taught them the way of humility and divine love.

Christ was reduced to a servant in order that God will have His way and exalt Him later. Servant-hood which is a seed faith, is regarded as the only prerequisite for Christian leadership and advancement. To abide in His Shadow, you have to emulate His characteristics and attributes. He said in Matt. 5:48, Serving also means ministering with love and compassion to the needs of those who require help without you expecting any reward, since God rewards the seed faith of service. It also means stooping as low as the situation demands.

Moses tended the flocks of his father-in-law (Ex. 3:1); Joshua served Moses as his assistance (Ex. 24:13, Josh. 1:1); David served Saul (1 Sam.16:21). The end of these exercise of service from the bottom line, resulted in notable upgrading of progress and prosperity which justified it. Seed faith can give rise to financial breakthrough, healing, outstanding performance in a competitive exam, appointment to a privileged position, deliverance and growth into a state of spiritual maturity, etc.

Jesus cautioned that you cannot put new wine into an old wine skin or else it will burst. In the scriptures good and evil cannot exist together. Faith and grace cannot operate in legalism. If Christ has justified you as righteous, you are no longer subject to the law.

When you sow, you are advised to do so meaningfully, bountifully, painstakingly and with love, so that you can reap the full measure. When you sow the fruit of the Spirit it may not seem easy, but with perseverance and faith the Holy Spirit will make everything possible.

If you are at the top position already, check to make sure that you are positioned on the right foundation. If you are at the bottom and striving to do His Will, have faith that Jesus will propel you safely upwards through the help of the Holy Spirit. This chapter ends with the quotation on Lk. 6:20-21, which shows that the end will justify the suffering you pass through in the process to abide in His Shadow. It reads:

"Blessed be you the poor, for yours is the kingdom of God.

Blessed are you that hunger now, for you shall be filled.

Blessed are you that weep now, for you shall laugh."

DIVINE LOVE IN HIS SHADOW

Love is regarded as the most important requirement and is what Christ talked about in Jn 15:13. *"Greater love has no man than this, that a man should lay down his life for his friends."* Some believers may not fully have understood the extent to which the practice of this love goes. I may not be an exception to this. The Lord once sent His spiritual messengers to ask me how like Jesus I am. He said that His judgement will be based on this. It is described in Songs of Sol. 8:6 as being stronger than death. Christ had to die for man because His love for God and for man was stronger than death. God's love for man was so strong that He did not mind passing His only begotten Son through the excruciating pain of death in order to save mankind from condemnation and the second death.

We are warned to be extremely careful in our exercise of divine love, because God Himself is love. 1 Jn 4:16 clearly states, *"God is Love."*

The book of 1 Cor.13, explained in details the uniqueness and overwhelming importance of the divine love which Jesus came to teach mankind. Both the gifts of the Spirit and the fruits of the Spirit have to be exercised and lived out in divine love. The Holy Spirit Himself will make you aware of the Love of God for you. You can say that Love is the foundation on which the fruits and the gifts of the Spirit are worked out. It is like the thread that holds the fabric of Christianity together, and a trademark of Christ the Lord.

Thoughts of evil, resentment, anger, bitterness and such like, drive away love. Love has many attributes and endurance is one of them. Endurance and love are required for victory in the following instances: When you have lost regard and esteem because people have misunderstood your meekness and humility as a lack of strength; when nobody asks your opinion or tells you the truth anymore; when you are denied your rights and made to suffer unnecessary mockery because of your righteousness; when you are trying to spread the gospel, and the only response you are getting from unbelievers is criticisms and persecution; when you are discriminated against by fellow believers as a result of your refusal to compromise the Word in certain areas.

One's relationship to others should be based on the divine love of God. It should reflect humility, service and compassion. It demands that we love our enemies and pray for them; prefer others to ourselves, and not be judgemental. If we do not have love, we cannot pray for our enemies. While we were yet sinners Christ died for us (Rom. 5:8). It is required of us, however difficult it may seem, to try to love our enemies and pray for them.

Do not stand aloof from the problems of your enemies especially at those times when the love of God reveals that your help is needed. The true enemy of divine love is self. All the selfish attributes of man has to die before the true love of God can get out and be rightly extended to others. Self restricts the practice of love. Bitterness, unforgiveness, selfishness, pride, envy, covetousness, anger and the likes are all hedges against love.

Through the way Christ lived his life, the disciples were able to understand and appreciate the practice of love as it relates to service and humility. It is only a heart that is filled with love that can develop the humble desire to serve.

Sincere love flows from the heart, and God is always able to recognise and make distinctions between genuine and insincere love (1 Pet. 1:22). We are children of God because we love each other the way Christ loves us. If the world does not perceive that quality in us, then we are not children of God and cannot be able to win souls or reproduce for him.

The Love of God is referred to as the bond of perfection. It is the platform on which the life of a Christian is standing. God's love is sacrificial, unconditional, enduring, selfless, caring, everlasting, faithful, and forgiving to say the list. One of the reasons Jesus came to live on this earth, was to teach and demonstrate the love of God, as opposed to our own manner of love which is based on self and circumstances. When we walk in the love of God, then our walk with the Lord will be stable and successful.

A significant aspect of how you succeed in climbing that tree of holiness to His Shadow, and how you can continue to remain there depends on how you exercise your love for God and for man; and on how successfully you resolve conflicts with people, especially in a situation of diverse opinions and perspectives. Love is like cholesterol that binds together; like salt that makes the food palatable. Anything done, spoken or conceived without love, becomes unscriptural. It will not glorify God and will never advance your walk with Him. If you do not give your tithes and offerings with love, you have not really given anything.

Mk 12:30-31 places the Love of God highest in the rating of other virtues, and reads; *"And you shall love the Lord your God, with all your heart, with all your soul, with all your mind and with all your strength. This is the first commandment."* And the second is like it, which is this; *"You shall love your neighbour as yourself. There is no other commandment greater than these."*

The second is as a result of the first. It is through loving and obeying God and His Son Jesus Christ, that you can develop and practise same love for your neighbour (1 Jn 4:21). The love of God makes it possible to appreciate other people's problems and to offer any help we can render.

If your kindness is not extended out of love, it creates a strained relationship. Jesus gave His life as a ransom for man in love. He never complained although we know that He was made to experience a very painful period of torture. He died still loving those who killed Him. This was why He asked us to love our enemies and bless those who curse us.

1 Cor. 13:3 states; *"And though I bestow all my goods to feed the poor, and though I give my body to be burnt, but have not love it profits me nothing."* The difference between our type of giving and the sacrifice at the Cross, is the willingness and love attached to the sacrifice. This also applies to the tithes, offering, first fruits and all such things that we present to God in the Church. It should not be perceived as a compulsion. Anything we give to God without love may not attract any reward; likewise any sacrificial gift we render for personal recognition, will attract zero reward because we have already received the reward from the people.

A life that has no love for others cannot grow spiritually. When we live and move in divine love, it is easier for the Holy Spirit to operate in us. Christ is the Symbol of God's love and the fulfilment of all righteousness.

The love of man should be like the love of Christ which is not partial. Peter in Acts 10:34-35 says; *"For I know of a truth that God is no respecter of persons; but in every nation, whoever fears Him and does what is righteous is acceptable to Him."* The love of Christ is free and truthful towards all.

There are many examples of those who truly demonstrated divine love in the scriptures. In interceding for the sinful Israelite, Moses pleaded with God and said in Ex. 32:32 *"But now, if You will only forgive their sin, but if not, blot me out of the book that You have written."* There was also the poor widow, who parted with the last farthing she had in order to give to God; Stephen who prayed for his killers that God would forgive them. David restrained himself from slaying Saul who was pursuing him for slaughter when God led David to where Saul was sleeping helplessly. All these people acted selflessly and out of love according to the scripture in Gal. 6:2.

THE SPIRITS OF THE LAST DAYS

What are the spirits of the last days and how are they impacting on the effort of man to abide in the Shadow of the Almighty? There are positive spirits as a result of the end time outpouring of the power of God on man (Joel 2:28-29). There are also the negative spirits which the Bible refers to as the spirits of the antichrist which is spoken about in 1 Jn 4:3 and When man abides successfully in the Shadow of the Almighty, he is in a much assured position to defeat the negative impact of the spirits of the antichrist, which are the spirits of the last days.

2 Tim. 3:1-5, 7 reads: *"But know this, that in the last days, perilous times will come. For men will be lovers of*

themselves, lovers of money, boasters, proud, blasphemers, disobedient to parents, unthankful, unholy, unloving, unforgiving, slanderers, without self-control, brutal, despisers of good, traitors, headstrong, haughty, lovers of pleasure rather than lovers of God, having a form of godliness but denying its power" Always learning and never able to come to the knowledge of the truth."

Assuredly, the Word of God in Jer. 32:27 says: *"Behold I am the Lord, the God of all flesh. Is there anything too hard for Me?"* The present trend of the antichrist spirit foretells of what Christ refers to as the time before the great tribulation, which is the seven years of intense suffering and anguish for man on this earth as prophesied in Dan. 12:1. This will be before the sudden arrival of Christ into the world again. The intention of these spirits is to divert man's heart away from obeying the will of God his Creator. They have created distractions in the form of worldly enticements that are fed by the lust of the flesh.

These days are characterised by many unusual happenings as foretold also by Jesus in the book of Matt. 24:7-12 which reads: *"For nation will rise against nation, and kingdom against kingdom. And there will be famines, pestilences, and earth quakes in various places. All these are the beginning of sorrows. Then they will deliver you up to tribulation and kill you, and you will be hated by all nations for my Name's sake. And many will be offended, will betray one another, and will hate one another. Then many false prophets will rise up and deceive many. But he who endures till the end shall be saved. And this gospel shall be preached in all the world as a witness to all the nations, and then the end will come."*

Endurance will lead to abiding in His Shadow. The gospel is also currently being preached through different media to the world. All these prophecies have already come to pass. Isa. 24:5-6 stated that man would be responsible for all the woes that would come upon the world at this time. It reads; *"The earth also is defiled under the inhabitants thereof; because they have transgressed the laws, changed the ordinance, broken the everlasting Covenant. Therefore hath the curse devoured the earth, and they that dwell therein are desolate."* Read carefully these words of prophesy and meditate on them with regards to what is happening today. The book of Revelations which is an exposition of the tribulations of man when the wrath of God shall come says in chapter 16:3 *"And the second angel poured out his vial upon the sea: and it became as the blood of a dead man: and every living soul died in the sea."* Verse 9 talks of men being scorched by a great heat. Rev.16:18 reads: *"And there were voices, and thunders and lightning; and there was a great earthquake, such as was not since men were upon the earth. So mighty an earthquake and so great"*

These devastating prophecies and revelations, coming from Jesus Christ Himself to us through John His apostle, were not heeded and those that have not yet happened will surely be fulfilled. Man is trying to solve spiritual problems through physical scientific means rather than the spiritual through which they were foretold. This perspective ignores the Word of God that embodies solutions to all the problems. It also makes no provision in the heart of man to fear and reverence God His Creator. Js 2:19 says: *"Thou believest that there is one God; thou doest well. The devils also believe and tremble."* Do you believe and also fear God? The sceptic and evolutionists of today no longer believe in the Word of God, and as a result do not fear and reverence God. They lack the knowledge of the Word of God, which is the spiritual that guarantees the physical.

Can a layman perform a medical operation to heal the sick? The more knowledgeable one is about any problem, the better equipped that person can be to deal with it. Today we are beset with the following problems, which may worsen appreciably. A state of unstable economy, diseases that defy medication, unpredictable weather changes giving rise to global warming, droughts, sea level rising and overflowing, fires, earthquakes, persecution of Christians, killings, wars and violence, spiritual and physical immorality as a result of changes in the marriage institution and family structure, political upheavals, uprisings and in some countries suppressive government. These experiences have established the validity of Biblical prophecies. Scripturally speaking, it is believed that no technology, social custom, philosophical findings, resources or human wisdom can withstand the tide of these unusual problems. Only repentance, faith in Jesus, and obedience to the Word of God can draw out the mercy of God to reverse their movement if He so desires. This is why Jesus calls it the beginning of sorrows for man. It is expected that Christ will arrive to put all things right, after judgement. He will get rid of the old and replace it with what is right. The book of Revelation prophesied that there will be a new heaven and a new earth. Isa. 65:17.

The end time spirits of the antichrist have given rise to

various perspectives on the validity of man as man and woman as a woman. People have convinced themselves that they can now convert to whatever sex they want irrespective of what they are born to be. This has seriously affected the marriage institution, mode of dressing and compromised the established family structure. This change will be further explored, including this state of moral and spiritual decay on the life of man in another chapter.

If there is any reason to doubt these prophecies, why then are they being fulfilled today? In September 2018, a divine figure appeared to me as I prayed in the very early hours of the morning. He said that very soon strange things that had not happened before, will soon begin to happen in the world. He emphasised the need for all to align their character to that of Christ. It can also be said that this is a time when people prefer to conceal their real views rather than express them openly. It is also a period of shameless sexual child abuse, both physically and spiritually; an age of increased suicidal tendencies, killings, and violence.

Heb.12:2 reads: *"Looking unto Jesus, the author and Finisher of our faith."* In order to establish a good conviction of this faith, it is necessary to have sufficient knowledge of the one you repose your faith on. This is why the Bible says that faith comes by hearing the Word of God, and also by reading it. The Word that you read or hear and then meditate on, goes in and challenges the old nature of sin in your life. This gives rise to conviction, repentance and faith. The more you read and listen to it you will come to a good understanding of God's power, love, and holiness, and the need to seek His help. Your faith will grow.

Some people question the existence of God by claiming that they do not believe in the existence of a Higher being Who created the entire universe; and that the Bible was compiled by man. This they do because they lack the knowledge and understanding of the Word. Any decision that is based on ignorance does not reflect the Truth. They forget that most of the books of the New Testament were written by those men who closely lived and worked for Christ and were inspired by the Holy Spirit.They were eye witnesses of all that He did. Most of us who originally did not make time to read the Word of God well, our reading of it being always hurried, also rebelled against its application in our lives. But when we repented and made time to sturdy it, its truth, power and benefits began to be immediately appreciated.

Any decision that is based on human intellect alone is opposed to the Will of God. The environmental problems are threatening to get out of control. Man can only do what is humanly possible; the eventual outcome depends on God. (Lk.1:37). He, Who created the entire world through Christ, the spoken Word, is the One Who also controls and regulates everything He created (Gen.1:1-24, 2:7; 2:21; Ps. 24:1-2; etc). All His creations are subject to Him and His Son Jesus through the Holy Spirit. Jesus walked on the sea Matt. 14:2-5. On another occasion He commanded the waves to cease and they immediately obeyed Him because they knew Him, Who created them Matt. 8:24-26. God parted the Red Sea to allow the Israelites to escape from their enemies and to destroy Pharaoh and his army. Ex.14:28-29. He alone can speak peace into the environment He created.

The Word of God in Rom. 1:20 says; *"For since the creation of the world, His invisible attributes are clearly seen, being understood by the things that are made, even His eternal power and Godhead, so that they are without excuse."* All the evidence of the existence of God and His creative power can be seen in the trees, seas, animals, sun, moon,

77

stars, sky, mountains, earth, heaven, rain, the weather, man and life, etc. He created and regulates them. These testify to His Great Power and Might. To abide in His Shadow one must believe according to Ps. 24:1 that *"The whole earth is the Lord's and the fullness thereof; the world and all who dwell therein. For He has founded it upon the seas, and established it upon the rivers."*

The whole of Genesis chapter one is about how God created the heaven and the earth. Verses 1-4 reads *"In the beginning God created the Heaven and the earth. And the earth was without form and void; and darkness was upon the face of the deep. And the Spirit of God moved upon the face of the waters. And God said let there be Light and there was Light. Gen. 2: 7 reads. "And the Lord God formed man of the dust of the ground and breathed into his nostrils the breath of life; and man became a living soul."* All these evidence the existence of an overall God of Mighty Power Who commands and controls in love and humility.

The Bible says in Ps. 16, that *"In His Presence is fullness of joy, at His Right Hands are pleasures for evermore."* When you abide in His Shadow, although you do not see Him, it is as good as being in His presence. Ps. 27:5 says, *"For in the time of trouble He shall hide you in His pavilion. In the secret place of His tabernacle shall He hide you."*

The book of Rom.1:25 describes this age as a time *"when people exchanged the Truth of God for a lie and worshiped and served the creature rather than the Creator, Who is blessed for ever. Amen."* It is a period when evil is publicly proclaimed as good and good as obsolete; a period when some are trying to rewrite the Bible to suit the laxity and moral decadence of the age. Those who do so, are hailed as heroes. 1 Cor. 1:18 says that the Word of God is foolishness to the ignorant, but to those who believe, is the power of God unto Salvation. According to 1 Jn 4:1-3, the many spirits of the antichrist that have gone out into the world to deceive mankind, have produced many diverse religious and none religious beliefs and practices. These teach contrary doctrines which are in direct opposition to the Word of God. The Word stands for truth and unity and is settled in heaven. It is the hedge which God gave to mankind for unity and protection.

These changes have given rise to different perspectives on the way God's ordained life that will usher one into His Shadow should be lived; the way people are supposed to relate to each other in love, modes of dressing biblically ordained family patterns, etc.

MAINTAINING GOD'S STANDARDS

God's standard of righteousness requires that we live in obedience to His will, exercise faith in the Lord Jesus Christ, and love others as ourselves. This is living according to the Divine Nature of God. This will make it possible for one to abide peaceably under His Shadow. Ps.16:11 says: *"...in His Presence is fullness of joy, at His Right Hand are pleasures for evermore."* God's standard of goodness is perfect. He preached the need for that perfection to Abraham in Gen.17:1 in order to get His promises fulfilled in His life. He said, *"I am The Almighty God; walk before Me, and be thou perfect."*

Jesus radiates God's standard of goodness in whatever He says or touches, and wherever His presence is felt. The

Light of God Which is the Light of Life shines through Him, and is also transferable with its power into humans. Those who are under His Shadow are covered by that Light. In Matt. 9:22 when the woman with the issue of blood touched His garment, virtue in that light went out of Him into her and she was healed instantly. When all the sick in Gennesaret were brought out to Him, as many as touched the hem of His robe, received the light of the same anointing and were healed. In Acts 19:12 handkerchiefs and aprons taken from Paul were given to the sick and they were healed. Although men do not see Him today, such miracles can still be received through faith and serious prayers. Jn 14:12-14, Js. 5:15-16.

Ps. 24:3-5 reads: *"Who shall ascend into the hill of the Lord? Who shall stand in His holy place? Only he who has clean hands and a pure heart. Who has not lifted his soul unto evil, no sworn deceitfully. He shall receive the blessing from the Lord, and vindication from the God of His Salvation."* God is a perfectionist and demands absolute holiness and righteousness. He relates to man on the basis of a covenant relationship for we humans, cannot be trusted. Is. 26:10b says, *"...for when Thy judgements are in the earth the inhabitants of the world will learn righteousness."* To this end, He has determined the path which man has to follow in order to survive and make Heaven. Righteousness love and faith in Christ, are regarded as the foundation from which all thoughts, words and actions should proceed. This is the bases for all human relationships. This is the standard which God has set, which is to be attained through following the path of His Son Jesus Christ, Who is the Way, the Truth and the Life.

If you value and obey the Word, it will perform its duties in your life Ps. 107:20. Prov. 4:22. The extent to which one compromises the Word is relative to the help that person will receive from it. A weak attitude of touch and go, or a lack of concentration may not release the power of the Word into one's life. Jesus said, "Let your yes be yes and your no be no." This perspective is clean and needs no further embellishment. You have to believe in the truth to be able to practise it. If you are set on manipulating the truth in order to make it seem easier and interesting, you have made the Word of God which is settled in Heaven untrue and unscriptural. The book of 1 Jn 3:23 has also summarised this righteousness by saying; "*And this is His Commandment, that we should believe in the Name of His Son Jesus Christ, and love one another as He gave us commandment.*"

Unfortunately man has rebelled against God's standard of righteousness and instituted his own modified or opposing standard, which he finds easier and more interesting to keep. Jesus is the beginning and the end of all the righteousness that the law demands. One of the reasons why most young believers do not realise what the standard of God's righteousness requires, may be attributed to the fact that the process of sanctification was not appreciated. The response after being born again is often different from what happens years after. At that moment you are born again there is a sudden realisation of the truth of what is required. As time goes on, the daunting realisation that the journey may be far from easy sets in.

It is at this point that those who have not kept a steady pace in the reading studying and practice of the Word, begin to indirectly modify its standard to suit theirs. This makes the attainment of grace difficult. Prov. 24:10 says. *"If you faint in the day of adversity, your strength is small."* It is unfortunate not to determine to experience the real benefits of salvation; and very frustrating. Success largely depends on not giving up. Through the mercy of God, the Holy Spirit redirects one consciously to the reality of what is required. At this stage, the believer, out of panic and obviously fed up with trying to modify the Word, intensifies his efforts in the reading, studying, understanding and living the Word. Determination without action cannot attract the strength of God. It is like sanctification without practice. When the Holy Spirit comes to help, allow Him to settle on and bless the likeness of Christ in you. It is the righteousness of Christ in you that will keep the Holy Spirit alive in you. Do not quench the Spirit. When the panic is gone one settles down and sincerely prays to cooperate with the Holy Spirit, and to allow Him to guide and lead him into the Shadow of God.

In our quest to abide under the Shadow of the Almighty, it becomes imperative that we should conform to God's standard since man can neither lead God their Creator, nor be able to lead themselves. God will judge man according to His own standard and expects him or her to prepare and attain that standard, while on this earth. The purpose of this chapter is to remind us of how far we might have deviated from God's standard and the need to allow ourselves to be revived and strive towards it through the help of the Holy Spirit. It will start by showing some scriptural passages that reveal God's standards and try to offer some explanations considered relevant to their application.

Some Standards Specified By God

Abiding in God's grace will make it possible to attain God's standard. This is possible through faith and obedience to the Holy Spirit and the scriptures. Man is also supposed to believe in His creative miraculous powers, even in the face of impossible situations.

Matt. 7:21 reads: *"Not everyone who says to Me Lord Lord, shall enter the kingdom of heaven, but he who does the Will of my Father in Heaven."* The Will of God is that with faith in the Lord Jesus man shall live righteously and in the divine love of God. The Holy Spirit will release God's power that will quicken ones desire, discipline determination and strength to obey the Word. He also will empower the ability needed to say no to the flesh. This is subject to man's cooperation and obedience. The standard of God is to be attained also by grace and not by works of righteousness alone.

A standard of God's righteousness can be found in Js 2: 10 which reads: *"For whoever shall keep the whole law, and yet stumble on one point, he is guilty of all."* Put your faith in Christ, the Author and Finisher of your faith. Follow and obey Him. You have to know Him in order to do this. If you slip, apologise immediately and strive to make amends. We are all in this struggle through the power of the Holy Spirit.

Matt 7:24-27 reads *"Therefore whoever hears these sayings of mine and does them, I will liken him to a wise man who built his house on the rock; and the rains descended and the floods came and the winds blew and beat on that house; and it did not fall, for it was founded on the rock. But everyone who hears these sayings of Mine, and does not do them, will be like a foolish man who built his house on the sand; and the rain descended, the floods came, and the winds blew and beat on that house, and it fell, and great was its fall."*

It is not really easy to build on a rock. This requires a lot of work. The rocks need to be painstakingly cut into the right sizes and positioned properly before being cemented. It is a laborous exercise that demands patience and hard work. So also is living holy in Christ Jesus. 2 Tim.3:12 states that those who live godly in Christ Jesus shall suffer persecution. Most people build their houses on the sand. Maybe because it is cheaper, easier and faster. These are the ones that go to great lengths to avoid the suffering and afflictions which are part of this world; and as a result indirectly enter into agreement with the evil one, who will eventually pull down both them and their houses, signifying physical and spiritual death.

Jesus warned in Eph. 5:27 that He is coming to rapture a Church without spot or wrinkles, i.e. without any stain of sin in order to qualify as His bride. This mirrors the perfection of God's standard. This is not an impossibility to God Whose Spirit can make it possible. Most importantly God is also merciful, loving and forgiving to His children. Determination, self-control and consistency, are needed in order to follow the ways of God.. We believe that with God all things which are impossible with men, are possible. Luke 1:37. Even as you are walking under His Shadow, problems are bound to arise because they are part of the ups and downs of life. Ps. 23:4.

In Jn 15:1-2 Jesus said, *"I am the true Vine and My Father is the Vine Dresser. Every branch that does not bear fruit He removes. Every branch that bears fruit He prunes to make it bear more fruit."* This shows that God is in support of total cleansing. Just as He insisted that the Israelites of old should cleanse themselves before coming near the tabernacle to present and offer their sacrifices to him, so He is telling us today to cleanse our hearts of sin before coming to Him; to present our bodies as instruments of righteousness to Him.

Long suffering is a fruit of the Spirit. The Church in Smyrna which Jesus congratulated for doing well, was also warned by Him that the enemy would be bringing more problems their way. It was not as if He was not able to withhold the problems as a result of their exemplary good behaviour; but God's standard has to be met. Zech. 13:9 reads: "*And I will bring the third part through the fire and will refine them as silver is refined and will try them as gold is tried: they shall call on My Name and I will hear them*" There is need for man to willingly accept the fellowship of Christ's suffering as one makes the sacrifice of righteousness.

God has given the believer power and authority over the enemy both spiritual and physical in Mk 16: 17-18, Lk 10:19. Matt. 16:19, Matt. 18:18-20. This authority is expected to be exercised according to His standards. Authority in the Church is exercised in an attitude of childlike humility, and servant like service to others. In the world authority is through domination and control. Jesus is saying that authority should be exercised in the following manner. It should not be used to earn public recognition and praise. It should not be exercised for self-interest or gain. It should not be used to intimidate or to dominate others. It should not be used to compromise the Word of God. It should not be used to terminate human life. Jesus did not kill anybody when He lived on this earth. It should be used only to pray, bless, teach, deliver, heal, protect, glorify God, serve and obey the Word. It should be used in love, humility, and to win souls for God.

In Matt. 5:28 is one of God's standard of righteousness. It says that looking at a woman to lust for her is regarded as a sin of adultery or fornication. This sin like every other sin, needs to be repented of, confessed before God, forgiven and remitted; for one to be able to abide in His Shadow.

In Matt. 12:36, it is written that a man shall give account of every idle word they speak in the day of judgement. Math. 5:37 warns that your yes shall be yes and your no shall be no. The purpose is to make one not to speak negatively about another, and to think only good thoughts. Bad thoughts open doorways for the evil one to enter the body. The truth does not require any discolouration. To practice the Truth one has to understand it too. Matt. 5:39 states; *"But I say unto you that ye resist not evil; but whosoever shall smite thee on thy right cheek turn to him the other cheek also."* Man is not supposed to retaliate, but to defeat evil with good because of the New Covenant of love and grace.

Heb. 8:10 states that God has already put His laws in man's mind and written them in their hearts so that it will be easier for them to live in obedience. This has to do with having a good knowledge of the Word of God and the in dwelling of the Holy Spirit in the heart of believers in order to transform them into true children of God. He will nurture in them the desire and power to appreciate the sacrifice at the Cross, to understand and remember the Word of God, guide and protect etc. Obedience is as a result of faith. You have come to a good understanding of Him from His Word. The result should be obedience through Love. Any obedience without love is questionable.

Matt. 7:12 reads: *"Therefore whatsoever you will that men should do to you, do ye so unto them. For this is the law and the prophets."* You meet a homeless man lying on the pavement, you have no money in your purse, or might have given what you had out. Do not express sympathy and move off. Speak some comforting and reassuring words to him or pray briefly and plead the blood of Jesus on him. He needs some practical expression of Christ's Love from you.

According to Matt. 7:22-23, the use of the authority of the scriptures and the power of the Name of Jesus to perform miracles will not necessarily qualify any to enter the Kingdom. The righteousness of the heart that comes through faith and love is more important. Jesus is asking believers today whether they are actually doing better than unbelievers; seeing that some of the unbelievers also fear God, love those who love them, obey their authority, pray fervently to their gods, give generously, work extremely hard, are also humble and not quarrelsome in their own ways. They try to be at peace with their fellow unbelievers. God's standard is that believers should do all these and more. They should love their neighbours as themselves and obey the Lord Jesus Christ with a pure heart, sincere faith, and a clear conscience.

Jesus focus is on pleasing others rather than oneself. In

Rom. 15:3, He said; *"The reproaches of those who reproach you have fallen on me."* It is written also in Gal. 6:2 *"Bear each other's burden, and you will fulfil the Laws of Christ."*

Isa. 26:3 reads: *"Thou will keep him in perfect peace whose mind is stayed on Thee because he trusts in Thee."* If your thoughts are focused only on God you will hardly think evil. In Eph. 2:10 Paul the apostle said that you should think only of what is good and true not of anything bad and evil, for we are created to do good. If you abide in the Shadow of the Almighty, the Holy Spirit will help you to focus your thoughts on the things of God which is God's standard for you.

Matt. 6:22-23 says *"The light of the body is the eye. If therefore thine eye be single, thy whole body shall be full of light. But if thine eye be evil, the whole body shall be full of darkness."*

There is a need for one to manage their eyes so that they do not lead them into temptation. Avoid negative tempting sights, wasteful things that are of no benefit to the soul and spirit; anything that is against the Word of God; for they open doorways that lead to temptation. Under His Shadow, you will hardly have time for those things.

There are some instances where Gods standard may not be easily understood although in the end it is right. This is because His ways are not our ways and He foresees the end from the beginning. He uses the uneducated, the lowly, the despised, the poor the repentant sinners, to show that high standards of conduct and achievement can be attained by any who is humble, willing to follow Christ and obedient to the Word. His Kingdom is not restricted to the privileged. In Mal. 1:2-3 before birth God preferred Jacob to Esau. In Eph.3:6, He called the Gentiles who are not His people to be fellow heirs with Christ. In 1 Sam.16:7, 13, David the youngest of his siblings was anointed King. In Gen.45:4-5 Joseph the second youngest of twelve children was sent ahead to go and prepare a place for the Israelites in Egypt. In Matt. 26:9-13, 28:1. Mary who had a problem of sexual immorality became an ardent disciple of Christ. Jn 4:28-30, the adulterous woman Jesus met at the well became a soul winner in her town. Hos.1:2-3, Hosea married a harlot in order to satisfy God's standard. In Josh. 2:9-14, Rahab the prostitute in Jericho became a saint.

All these people acted in obedience to the Will of God. They were all elected and attained God's standard by grace.

Man's Standard

Man devices and follows his own standard of righteousness for many reasons. There is the impression that God's standard is unattainable, in view of the suffering and length of time involved in trying to maintain it. This erroneous view ignores the advice in Lk. 1:37 which states that with God all things are possible. This is when one reposes implicit trust in Him. Man's standard is considered far easier, relaxing, more interesting and suited to the world values which human flesh craves for.

New technology has created a great diversion from the Word of God. Human intellect which is in direct opposition to the Word tends to institute rules and regulations contrary to the wisdom of God. Most unbelievers tend to play down on the scriptural proof and significance of Christ's Messiahship, as is shown in His birth, baptism, miracles, signs and wonders, crucifixion, resurrection and second coming. Lack of faith is another reason. Jesus told the Pharisees and Scribes, that if they did not believe Whom He was, they should then believe Him at least for the works that He had done. Jn. 14:11. Without faith in Christ one is no better than the scribes and Pharisees of the Old Testament who believed only in the laws of Moses. Those who are still guided by the law, will experience problems with most of the New Testament requirements that demand that you go two miles with him who wants you to go a mile with him. If anyone smites you on one cheek turn to him the other. If anyone wants your coat, let him have your cloak also. Matt.5:39-41. If you live according to the ways of the world, which ways Jesus has already defeated at the Cross, you can not dwell in His Shadow. When the problems attendant to that life style arise, Christ may not be able to relieve your sufferings. Maybe if you genuinely repent, and continue in prayers, he can be merciful.

When man is under very serious attack by the enemy, man is restricted to the use of the weapons of warfare which God made available to him in Eph. 6:11-18. Matt 5:44 reads: *"Pray for your enemies, bless them that curse you."* We all have to form this uneasy habit and not pray that any evil will come to them when the attack gets too hot. We can pray to have the Holy Spirit convict them of their sins so that they can repent. There are spiritual enemies who cannot repent. This is a challenge which every believer has to come to terms with. I have experienced a case where the believer prayed for the enemy because of the love for Christ. The enemy survived but has never really stopped attacking the believer. The grace of God who has the power to protect is needed here because they have passed the stage of recognising the consequences of their continuous action. Also ask Him to give them the spirit of conviction and repentance. Your praying for your enemy does not mean that God will terminate their lives suddenly the way they wanted to do to you. The Word of God states that because the punishment for sin is not executed immediately, the man of sin may continue to live in sin for some time, Ecc. 8:11. God always has His good reasons for every decision He makes. Ps.37:9 states, *"For evil doers shall be cut off; but those that wait upon the Lord, they shall inherit the earth."*

The standard of man is to live in self-indulgence, and to allow the flesh to lust for the world and its sensual desires. As a result he cannot understand the things of God, because they are spiritually discerned. But as a carnal Christian, if he through the guidance of the Holy Spirit, mortifies the flesh so that it is considered dead, he will be spiritually alive and able to relate to God.

For some, their standard is that Christ has completed the battle at the Cross and all that one is required to do is to repent of their sins before God, give their lives to Christ and continue to live in faith, not minding the minor sins of life which to them are inevitable. They believe that they will eventually make heaven. This is the concept of once saved always saved. This idea is so neatly packaged that you see believers radiating with happiness because whatever happens, they believe that they will still make heaven. There are some who speak the language of the Bible, and can quote it but will completely dissociate themselves from the suffering that may arise as a result of the Word. They perceive suffering as avoidable. Some because they doubt the power in the Word, do not feel compelled to live it out. This type of Christianity cannot justify the precious price paid for it.

There is something that is often seriously overlooked, and as a result causes its own problems. In Matt. 11:12 we are told that *"from the days of John the Baptist until now, the Kingdom of Heaven suffereth violence and the violent taketh it by force."* This means that success needs greater determination, commitment, hard work, faith and a willingness to endure suffering, affliction and persecution. In Rev. 3:16, Jesus warned that He will vomit out of His mouth, those who are neither cold nor hot. Let us not forget that it is His strength that will make perfect our weaknesses and He has to strengthen those whose existing strength and persistence are weak and needs boosting up; not those who are spiritually asleep or dead. Man's standard is often to accept some aspects of the Word and pretend that the other aspects can be ignored and explained away. In the book of Matt. 5, 6 and 7 Jesus took some time to make a distinction between God's required standard and that of man.

As time goes on some believers may through the knowledge of the Word, come to the realisation of the true nature of Christ, and follow Him in faith and obedience so that the Holy Spirit can guide them out of the temptations. For some, this realisation of what the true standard of God is, can lead to panic and a stronger desire to become more serious in their adjustment to the truth. I am not exempt from this learning. There is a yearning at this stage, to be firmly positioned in the Shadow of the Almighty. Ps. 31:20 reads: *"In the cover of Your Presence you hide them, from the plots of men; You store them in Your shelter from the strife of tongues."*

The natural man seeks to please himself, not others. This is contrary to the ways of Jesus which is mutual forbearance, servant like leadership and love. Rom. 15:1 reads: *"We then who are strong ought to bear with the scruples of the weak, and not to please ourselves.*" This is supposed to be a model of relationship between believers. When your expectations of the standard of making heaven does not meet with that of God, you will continue to experience problems in your relationship with Him. It is you that definitely has to make the adjustment not God.

There are two believers namely A and B. Believer 'A' has a much lower standard of endurance and righteousness. He is always full of complaints about how people infringe on his rights. He has to stand on the bus most of the time. Sometimes the bus driver forgets to stop at his bus stops. In his work place he complains of the misdeeds of fellow workers and the oppressive schedule of duties. He is expecting an unrealistic situation in an unrealistic world.

Believer 'B' tries to be guided by God's standard, and has a good knowledge of the Word of God. He remembers what the Lord Jesus said in John 16:33. *"In the world you will have tribulation, but be of good cheer. I have overcome the world."* He lives by faith and has come to the realisation that to meet God's standard he has to serve others, endure all hardship, live humbly and extend love to all. He overlooks all provocations and is always willing to give up his seat to others. He has come to the realisation that unnecessary complaints negates the practice of faith and will not improve matters. He therefore endures insults and afflictions, ignores and moves ahead. He is fast improving in his walk with the Lord and revealing a tremendous spiritual growth.

Christ is asking you today: what have you really done better than the unbelievers, beyond believing that He is the Son of God Who died to atone for your sins and is able to lead you to heaven? In terms of showing love to your fellow human beings fear and reverence towards God, and denying the pleasures of the flesh, suffering hardship without complaint, and winning souls for Christ, how far have you gone?

The spirit of the antichrist has released enticements into the world system through different spiritual and physical network of communications in order to plague and distract those who are not grounded in the Word. This has created the type of moral laxity that is threatening to be worse than the one that prevailed in the days of Sodom and Gomorra.

Some people refuse to perceive the old covenant in the light of the new covenant of grace based on faith in the Lord Jesus, and love for God and for fellow human beings.

It is written in 1 Jn 3:23. *"And this is His commandments: that we should believe on the Name of His Son Jesus Christ, and love one another, as He gave us commandment."* The belief in Jesus should inform the way one thinks, speaks and acts. In the process of doing this, one will be obeying the 10 commandments and living according to the fruits of the Spirit in Gal. 5:22-23. In Jesus the old covenant of the law which stands for fear and separation, and the new which stands for faith, love and grace are united.

THE RIGHT PERCEPTION OF SIN

Sin Defined

Sin is a general and serious word used to describe any thought, speech, or action which is contrary to the Word of God. Here are five scriptural passages which when put together can give a definition of what sin stands for.

In 1 Jn.3:4 sin is said to be the transgression of the law. God gave the 10 Commandments to make the people realise what sin is. Js. 4:17 says that omitting to do that which you are supposed to do is a sin. This means omitting to apply the Word to the way you live your life. You might have forgotten or purposely ignored to do this. 1 Jn. 5:17 states that all unrighteousness is considered sinful. Instead of being guided by the

Word in order to act rightly, you follow the wrong way.

Rom.14:23 states that anything done without faith is sinful. This is also the lack of faith in the ability of Jesus as the Son of God to lead you out of that problem of sin. Prov. 24:29 states that any thought of foolishness is sinful. On what do you always base your thoughts on? Is it on the ways of God, or on the satanic demands of the flesh, fear, false imagination, lust, anger, hatred and covetousness?

From these definitions we can infer that sin is disobedience to the will of God and putting the demands of the flesh or the world first against that of the Spirit. It is a deadly spirit that stealthily sneaks into man through sinful acts, blocks progress, puts him into bondage, and stubbornly resists being ejected. It can only obey the blood of Jesus that defeated it with its mate, death, at the Cross of Calvary.

Need for A Right Perception of Sin

A greater part of the afflictions and suffering of man is as a result of sin; for the Word asks in 1 Pet. 2:13, *"Who is he that will harm you if you are followers of that which is good?"* In Ps.119:71 David said. *"It is good that I was afflicted so that I could obey the statutes of God."* Whoever moves from the arena of righteousness to that of sin, experiences either immediately or later some negative repercussions and sometimes agonising suffering depending on the gravity of the sin. This is because sin has established consequences. Man is supposed to put things right after the new birth, by practicing the process of righteousness in his life. This may not be easy since most people continue to be hindered by the evil one. We are all trying and praying for the mercy of God in this. Man should exert greater effort to pray out resisting Spirits.

One school of thought is of the view that although God forgives, He still allows man to pass through the problems and afflictions he man invited as a result of sin; so that he can fully realise what he will get the next time he sins. One can trace many instances of this in the Old Testament where He always extended help to those who repented and cried out to him for help. 2 Chr. 33:9-13. Jesus rightly said to the paralytic man He healed in Jn 5:14, *"Sin no more, lest a worse evil come upon you."* Sin is man's worst enemy on earth. God loves man, but hates the sin in him. Once one repents God relents and forgives and cancels the punishment He would otherwise have allowed Jon 3:8-10.

A right perception of sin will enable one to avoid it and gain access into and remain in the Shadow of the Almighty. We cannot claim to love God and sin at the same time. The psalmist says: *"Serve the Lord with fear, and rejoice with trembling. Kiss the Son, lest He be angry and you perish in the way, when His wrath is kindled but a little."* Fear, which is as a result of the appreciation of His Worth, gives rise to reverence and obedience. When one appreciates God's stand towards sin, and the extreme length He went to set the way to eradicate it from the life of man, then fear, reverence and obedience towards Him and hatred for sin will arise.

Sin is highly infectious and insidious and not supposed to be tolerated or compromised. It is the enemy that steals into man unexpectedly, and makes its presence habitual. Its final motive is the complete destruction of man's heart and body. It makes demand of blood for its payment irrespective of the fact that Christ has already made the payment with His own blood and also paid the ransom of those who would believe in Him. Sin is locked up in agreement with death, and supplies it with its victims. It is man's worst enemy on earth. God loves man, but hates the sin in him.

The whole purpose of life is to combat and avoid sin, and make man live a righteous life in the service of God. The one intention of sin is to cast man into hell. God's intention to get sin eradicated from the life of man can better be understood because of the high price of the blood of Jesus paid as a ransom for man. Because of His perfect Holiness, it is necessary that God should judge and condemn sin.

The first step out of sin towards salvation, is to come to a realization of how dangerous and destructive it is, and the fact that the prize for it has been paid for already, by the blood of Jesus. This realization often leads to immediate repentance. Sin is supposed to be repented of, confessed, forgiven and remitted. Man is not supposed to die with it because it will never enter heaven with it's victim. Both will be cast into a fire that never quenches; and may live there for ever. There is not much time left for man on this earth.

Why is it Difficult to Give Up Sin?

1. Sin can only depart through Christ Whom God sent to nail it to the Cross. Col.2:14. Man was born in sin Ps.51: 5, and before he became born again has already

formed a habit of living in sin; a habit that has to be replaced by righteousness after he has accepted Jesus as Lord and Saviour and has received the gift of the Holy Spirit.

2 Cor. 5:17. Some people tend to despair after a few attempt and ask questions like this, "Have you ever seen a sinless man before?" This shows a lack of faith and determination to appropriate the grace that will make it possible. Believers are never expected to give up.

2. Since salvation is by grace, some make half-hearted effort to depart from sin, while looking forward to the day when Jesus will arrive to grant a general amnesty to all believers because according to them, once saved is always saved. Js. 2:26 states that faith without works is dead. Some of the present generation of Christians do not consider the honest, frank advice of Paul the apostle as practicable in this age. Paul had posed a question that discredited the idea of once saved is always saved by asking in Rom. 6:1-2 *"Shall we continue in sin that grace shall abide. God forbid. How shall we that are dead in sin live any longer therein?"*

We make God a liar and Christ an actor. Paul decided to make the sacrifice of righteousness by denying the satanic cravings of the flesh and to teach how to live according to the fruits of the Spirit. He also in Phil. 3:7-8, decided to forget his past achievements and considered their loss as gain for Christ. This fact made it possible for him not to be distracted by the past. He also decided to set his mind only on what is good. This made it possible for him not to open doorways for sin to come into his thoughts. He preferred to abide in the joy of the Holy Spirit. He wore Jesus as a garment even in the fellowship of His suffering. These are tips that helped him to attain a high level of righteousness. This can no doubt be of immense encouragement to those who genuinely want to depart from sin. Although I am still learning through these, I have found them extremely encouraging in my efforts to depart from sin.

3. Many read the Word of God but only a few are serious in applying it to the way they speak, think or act. We shall succeed in this narrow way by His Grace. There is a need for one to soak themselves in the Word, sturdy, meditate practice what is learnt so that the heart can be purified and regenerated. Somebody said to Jesus, *"Blessed is the womb that gave birth to you, and the breasts that fed you."* But He replied. *"Blessed are those who hear the Word and do it."* Lk 11:27. It can be said that the person was thinking in the flesh while Jesus replied in the Spirit.

The reluctance to come to God truly repentant and in humility, honesty, holy fear and reverence, makes it difficult for one to be in His Shadow, and appropriate His power to deliver, protect, guide and to bless.

The consequences of obeying the Word, and disobeying it are well stated in Isa.1:19-20. *"If you are willing and obedient you shall eat the good of the land; but if you refuse, you shall be eaten by the sword. For the mouth of the Lord has spoken."* Man is seriously distracted by the flesh and the world. This point has been dealt with in the chapter on the degenerate moral values.

Scriptural Revelations Of Why All Sin Must Be Stopped

1. Js 2:10 states that if anyone obeys the whole law, and fails in one, he is guilty of all. Sin should be perceived as a whole. The right attitude of the mind is to be developed to avoid sin, since Satan blinds the minds of man in order to get him to sin. Every sin committed consciously and not repented of, separates man from God.

2. Eph. 5:27 states that at His second coming, Jesus wants to present His Church which is also His body, *"a glorious church, not having spot or wrinkles, nor any such thing,*

but that she should be holy and without blemish." Only the mercy of God will deliver from what goes on in a handful of Churches at this end time.

3. 1 Jn. 3:8 reminds us of the fact that he who sins is of the devil; for the devil sins from the beginning; And so the Son of God came from Heaven to destroy the work of the devil which is sin in man. Man therefore is no longer supposed to live in sin. It is doubtful if any Christian will consciously really like to be associated with the devil.

4. Heb. 10:26-27 reads: *"For if we go on sinning deliberately after receiving the knowledge of the truth, there no longer remains a sacrifice for sins but a fearful expectation of judgement, and a fury of fire that will consume the adversaries."* This emphasises the need for continuous repentance.

5. Rom. 8:2 states: *"For the law of the Spirit of Life in Christ Jesus has set you free from the law of sin and death."* This is the same Spirit that sanctifies believer's hearts and implants His fruits in them. He is the one who does the separation from sin which is the whole purpose of salvation.

6 . If we do not start early in life and as soon as possible to avoid sin, a sinful habit will be accumulated and this may not be easy to give up.

8. It is assumed that if one cannot live a holy life on earth,

that person cannot do so in heaven.

9. Sin can never rapture, for there is no place for it in haven; and anybody who is still not making any effort to remit it, will not be able to get in.

Something God cannot accept is that sin will be perceived as an inevitable part of life by some, instead of a poisonous and deadly disease that had already been taken care of. A genuine need to repent and flee from sin is followed by confession of same before God and a determined mind to separate from it. Every unrepentant sin, it has been said, blocks a relationship with God and His goodness.

The Concealed Sin

The concealed sins can prove more dangerous than the revealed, because they do not humiliate or disgrace the sinner. One is not in a hurry to get rid of them; but if death comes unawares they can cast one into hell fire. Examples include the following. You think you have given up anger but you still find it lurking inside. It comes from nowhere and influences your decisions. Serious prayers are needed for the strength to resist it. Always look out for it.

You are convinced that you have forgiven the one who wronged you, but you still make reference to the incident as an illustration when the need arises. That means you are still remembering.

You have not yet committed adultery or fornication in your life, but there is a tendency to lust, as and when the need arises.

You perceive yourself a hard working person in the house of God, and you not only want others to notice it, but you are always making comparisons of yourself with people who may be more spiritually advanced than you. Pride or self-esteem is living inside.

You are a chosen vessel of God, but your problem is that you sold out yourself unconsciously. You are being advised by the one who has no spiritual value in the eyes of God instead of solely by the Word of God. You have compromised your faith in God.

If one has to move upwards God's way, they must shed all their worldly appendages in the flesh as they will hinder spiritual growth. You are still enjoying certain worldly habits although a born again Christian; while telling people that Christianity is in the heart. Sin is also from the heart and comes from lust and disobedience.

The Bible calls sin a little leaven that leavens the whole part. It must be rejected at all costs. A divine messenger once said to me: "Once it is called sin, avoid it."

In concluding this chapter it can be said according to Ezek. 33:11, that God is not interested in the death of a sinner, but that he should repent and turn away from his unrighteousness. As far as He is concerned, He has gone to great lengths to make adequate provision for over thousands of years in order to enable man walk away from sin through His Son Jesus Christ. Anybody deliberately continuing in sin, will meet not His mercy, but God's wrath in the end.

Christ has fully paid for man's sins with His own innocent blood. Sin is a very dangerous ally in the sense that if it is not quickly ejected, it will surely lead the sinner to death. (Rom. 8:2) The length, agony and severity of human suffering as a result of serious acts of disobedience is enough to make man learn to avoid sin. After repentance there is the need to develop a habit of rejecting that sin. The Word of God makes us to understand that when we walk in the fruits of the Spirit, we shall be able to avoid the sinful demands of the flesh.

The flesh in Jesus was destroyed at the Cross, so that the flesh in man will also be destroyed through the new birth. The sacrifice of righteousness demands that the sin in the flesh should be made a sacrifice of for Christ. It is the Holy Spirit Who will empower our desire and willingness to live righteously; but He has to be obeyed, as He is in agreement with the Word which is the Will of God (Zech. 4:6).

There is hope for man in the sense that forgiveness is still available today. One of the mysteries of the kingdom is that however foul the sin is, with repentance, faith in the Lord Jesus and obedience, the cleansing blood is still available to wash it off. This offer of mercy enables people of different faith to repent and be led to salvation. Ps. 51:17 says, *"A broken and contrite heart Oh God, You will not despise."* Peter said in Acts 10:34-35, *"Of a truth I know, that God is not a respecter of persons; but in every nation, whoever fears Him and walks in righteousness, is acceptable to Him."* Jesus is the beginning and the end of all righteousness. God said in Heb.8:12, *"I will be merciful to their unrighteousness and their sins, and their lawless deeds I will remember no more."*

The fallen angels were before abiding in the Heavenly Shadow of God, which is His rest. They lived holy and in complete obedience to the Will of God. When they were deceived by the evil one, they broke their hedges by disobeying the Will of God and fell from their exalted positions. Who can believe that they produced offspring like demons after their fall? This fact teaches that sin is no respecter of persons. There has never been any human whose life was completely sinless. All came from a background of sin. This fact should encourage those who have not accepted Christ as Saviour to do so.

Each day goes hastily, and never returns. Do not allow it to disappear with a record of your sins. There are many Biblical men of old, who lived in a fearful expectation of sin and did not give any opportunity to the day to escape with their sins: Abraham, (Gen. 22:12, 16-18); David (1 Sam. 24: 4, 10-12); Paul (2 Cor.11: 23-25); Moses (Exodus 14:12-14); Job (Job.1:8); Daniel (Dan. 6:20-22); Isaiah (Isa. 20:3); Joshua (Num. 27:18-19); Hosea (Hos.1 :2-3); Mary the Mother of Christ, (Jon.2 :3-5); Cornelius (Acts 10:1-2); and also prophets like Samuel who spent his entire life serving God closely and Jeremiah, Ezekiel, and many others.

RECOGNISING EVERY NARROW WAY

The song writer wrote: *"Teach me my God and King, in all things Thee to see. And what I do in anything, to do it as for Thee."* Jesus is the narrow way, to be carefully discerned in everything we do, say or think. When we walk with the Lord we go on the narrow way. We shall get to His Shadow through this Way, and surviving depends on our continuing the same way. This fact brings to mind, the passage in Matt. 7:13-14 which reads; *"Enter by the narrow gate, for wide is the gate and broad is the road that leads to destruction, and there are many who go by it; because narrow is the gate, and difficult is the way which leads to life, and there are few who find it."*

There is a way to drive home a relevant point, to express

feelings of disapproval or hurt, tame an angry companion and even endure derision or abuse. This way does not necessarily have to be that of irritation, complaints, contention and strife. It is the Narrow Way; the Way of Christ which is the way of Love. Isa. 35:8, 9b reads: *"And a highway shall be there, and it shall be called the Way of Holiness; the unclean shall not pass over it."*

This road is neither wide enough to play around with, nor to allow one to get entangled with the distractions of this world. It is straight, focused and purposed for the Kingdom. It is an exclusive road which only the righteous can pass through, and this can only be achieved by the help of the Holy Spirit. One can easily get bruised going on this way, but the person will also pick up a lot of knowledge and understanding through these bruises (2 Tim.3:12). It is also through these bruises that one can learn the graces of humility, love, longsuffering, self-control, gentleness, faithfulness etc. Jesus suffered excruciatingly on this way on this earth in order to create an access through it for man. Obviously there is something that attracts the majority of people to the wide way. Maybe the untamed nature of humans, the perceived comfort of and the ease of it, and the many deceitful pleasures and fleshly indulgencies involved, which are but transient.

In Jn 14:6 Jesus reaffirms that He is the Way, the Narrow Way and the only way out of sin to Heaven and eternal life. When you obey Him (The Word), and develop His characteristics and attributes through the guidance of the Holy Spirit, you are truly walking in His way, and abiding in His Shadow. There is a narrow way of doing everything; the way to pray, read the Word, relate to God and man, work, think, feel, speak, render help, etc. Most of these ways will be discussed in this chapter and will be supported by scriptures. It is the responsibility of every Christian to recognise and follow them.

Why The Narrow Way?

Christ's intention of teaching and demonstrating this way, is to make it possible for man to be separated from sin, access God the Father, live according to His divine Love, and dwell in His glory. The world and its enticements, technology and its expansion, the flesh and its sensual lusts and desires, and most importantly, lack of the knowledge of the Word of God, have gradually shifted man's focus away from the narrow to the wide way. As a result, some have convinced themselves that there is no difference between the two ways. The perilous nature of this present time requires that man should step back into the narrow way in order to have God's mercy and grace still available. When you walk in the fruits of the Spirit, you are on the narrow way, and conforming to the true likeness of the image of the Son of God.

The Narrow Way in Our Prayers

Matt. 7:7 reads: *"Ask and it shall be given you; seek and ye shall find; knock and it shall be opened unto you."* This answer is conditional to the fulfilment of God's requirements, which is the narrow way of praying. Asking requires faith and righteousness, seeking requires diligence and patience and knocking requires hard work and persistence. A relationship can be traced between the way we pray and the way we work. Praying rightly, energises our faith and determination to work hard.

Jn15:7 *"If you abide in me and my Words abide in you, you will ask what you will, and it shall be done for you."* This is praying through the narrow way; giving God back His Words relating to the request you are presenting. If you are not knowledgeable about the Word of God, you will not know what scriptures to quote in order to enhance your request and it may not be according to the

Will of God. Eph. 6:18 reads: *"...praying always with all prayer and supplication in the spirit"* This type of prayer is motivated and energised by the Holy Spirit.

Js 5:16 reads: *"The effective fervent prayer of a righteous man availeth much."* A prayer said earnestly in truth and by a righteous man, has more chances of achieving good results than any lukewarm praying or that of a sinner. Some years back, because I was feeling very tired I found myself praying in a weak and tired voice in the middle of the night. Suddenly a divine presence jolted me into reality by saying, "Open your mouth." This also was repeated on another occasion when I was praying in a very low voice. There are instances when we have to speak out. Hannah was muttering because she was overcome by sorrow and tiredness. The Priest misunderstood her. We also have to pray with reverence, humility, and love. The narrow way of prayer is also the way of praise, worship and intercession.

The Narrow Way in Our Work Life

When we sow the seed of hard work it yields a rewarding benefit. Christ worked tirelessly day and night. The narrow way is the way of honest laborious prayers and hard work. Serious prayers as demonstrated by Christ when He lived on this earth, sometimes requires hard work. Luke 22:43-44. Prov. 6:6 says; *"Go to the ant thou sluggard; consider her ways and be wise; which having no guide, overseer or ruler, provideth her meat in the summer, and gathereth her food in the harvest."* Lack of hard work leads to lack of fruitfulness and growth.

God does not delight in the poverty of His children Ps. 35:27. He wants them to work hard and get wealth which He Himself provides, so that they can bless others, that is, redistribute and live contentedly 2 Cor. 9:8. This purpose is based on the narrow way. A purpose that is based on covetousness, the pleasures of the flesh, pride, and worldly expansion of business and competition based on pride of success, is the broad way. Eph. 4:28 reads: *"Let him that stole steal no more; but rather let him labour working with his hands, the thing which is good, that he may have to give to him that needs."* The mind of every believer should be centred on this reason as they labour in their work. This is one reason God releases His blessings on believers, and not necessarily to cater for the needs of family and relatives alone, or to put aside massive extras for indulgence in pleasures.

Human Relationship

The purpose for all human relationships is to quietly market the love and goodness of Christ to others through the way we think, speak or act. Let those in authority and fellow workers perceive the love and goodness of Christ in the way you work and conduct yourself in your work place. This will definitely be as a result of a relationship based on peace, humility and love for others.

Our Feelings and the Narrow Way

The feeling that is as a result of any sinful desire of the flesh is not based on the narrow way. Any feeling which is in opposition to all lusts of both the flesh and the eyes and is directed by the Spirit of God is definitely the spiritual and the narrow way. A distinction has to be made between the two because the Word of God in Gal. 5:16 reads: *"Walk in the Spirit and you will not fulfil the lust of the flesh."* Having been justified, man is passed through a gradual process of sanctification by the Holy Spirit so that the flesh dies a natural gradual death and the Spirit can operate at full capacity. The mind is then purified. It is understood that only those who submit and respond successfully through this process of sanctification will continue to abide in the Shadow of the Almighty, and be glorified in the end.

Rom. 12:1 reads, *"I beseech you therefore brethren by the mercies of God that you present your bodies a living sacrifice, holy, acceptable unto God, which is your reasonable service."* Since Christ sacrificed His blood for man, man is supposed to sacrifice all the satanic demands that the flesh is making.

Ecc. 7:9 reads: *"Do not hasten in your spirit to be angry. For anger rests in the bosom of fools."* Once anger comes into any situation contention and strife will escalate, and love flees. Do not let your feelings and decisions be influenced or controlled by your anger. This is the wide way that leads to destruction. Recognise that anger is the little mad feeling that gradually wants to escalate into a rage, and mess you up. Strive to control your anger by exercising discipline, and resort to the Lord in prayers over the reason for it. This is the narrow way, referred to as the highway of holiness. Eph. 4:31-32 reads: *"Let all bitterness, wrath, anger, clamour and evil speaking be put away from you with all malice. And be ye kind one to another, and tender hearted, forgiving one another even as God for Christ's sake hath forgiven you."* Do not nurture any negative feelings in your mind. Try to forgive all, and when you forgive try to forget the offence just as God in Christ does. Heb. 8: *"For I will be merciful to their unrighteousness, and their sins and their iniquities will I remember no more."* We all are also trying to make a habit of this.

The Narrow Way in the Thought Pattern

When the mind is always focused on the Word of God, and not on the world, it is based on the narrow way. Rom. 12:2 reads: *"And do not be conformed to this world but be transformed by the renewing of your mind. The overwhelming need to get the mind changed after the new birth is established in these scriptures."* Heb. 8:10 reads: *"For this is the covenant that I will make with the house of Israel after those days, says the Lord. I will put my Laws in their mind and write them on their hearts; and I will be their God, and they shall be My people."* It is the intention of God to establish control over the heart of man, so that his thoughts will reflect His Word and Will. This covenant of grace between God and believers is effected by the indwelling of Holy Spirit in their minds and hearts. For this covenant to work, it is necessary that the mind is always focused on the things of the Spirit and not on that of the world or the flesh. The Holy Spirit is the inner light in man.

Ps. 24:4-5 reads *"He who has clean hands and a pure heart; Who has not lifted up his soul unto evil, nor sworn deceitfully. He shall receive the blessing from the Lord, and righteousness from the God of his salvation."* The clean hands and a pure heart, should be directed solely to obeying God. It is the Spirit that quickens the desires and purifies the hearts. This makes it possible to develop a broken and contrite heart acceptable to God.

Heb. 2:5-9 reads: *"Let this mind be in you, which was also in Christ Jesus. Who being in the form of God..... humbled Himself and became obedient to the point of even death of the cross."* What is special about childlike humility is that instead of demonstrating the fullness of the power which one can exercise without falling into sin, the person is perfectly content to live a life of servant-like and humble leadership. The heart of man is supposed to be meek and humble and preferring the needs of others first before self.

Matt. 6:21 says: *"Where your treasure is, there your heart will be."* Christ is supposed to be the treasure of all believing hearts. When your thinking is always selfish, acquisitive and based on the need to gratify the pleasures of life, then your treasure is your flesh and the world. This is the wide way that leads to destruction.

The Narrow Way in the Company We Keep

Eph. 5:11 reads: *"And have no fellowship with the unfruitful works of darkness but rather expose them."* Do not associate with them; you will either cover it, or take part in their evil ways. In 1 Cor. 5:9, Paul warned the Corinthian Christians not to keep company with sexually immoral people. In verse 11 he extended it to all the Christians who are sexually immoral or covetous, a reveller, idolater, drunkard, extortioner; not even to eat with them. As far as he was concerned these rules should be kept until genuine repentance is proved. Genuine repentance should be an indication that the person was ready to walk in the narrow way. One is however required to adopt a humble and compassionate attitude towards those who are struggling with these problems.

In the book of 2 Cor. 6:16-18 there is a similar distinction being drawn between the narrow and the wide way. This is one of the strongest scriptural statements about separating the good from the evil. All these things defile the body. The word of God states that whoever defiles the temple of God, will be destroyed by God 1 Cor.3:17. 1 Cor.15:33 states that evil company corrupts good manners.

The Narrow Way in Our conversation

When your speech reflects the Word of God, you will have a chance of abiding in His Shadow. You will be gentle and truthful in what you say, and will always speak words of love and encouragement. Gentleness is a fruit of the spirit. As you speak the Word in truth you will begin to experience the truth of the Word in your life.

Though the Word sanctifies, it also judges in the sense that it may not be fulfilled in your life if you are not walking on the narrow way. Jn 12:48 reads: *"He that rejected Me and receiveth not My Words, hath one that judgeth him: the Word that I have spoken, the same shall judge him in the last day."* Matt. 12:36-37 reads: *"But I say to you, that for every idle Word that a man may speak, they shall give account of it in the day of judgement. For by your Words you will be justified and by your Words you will be judged."* We have to repent of all the bad

Words we have spoken in the past and humbly ask God to have mercy and forgive us. There is also the need to pray for the empowerment to seriously determine to discipline the mouth. Eph. 4:29 reads, *"Let no corrupt word proceed out of your mouth but what is good, for necessary edification; that it may impart grace to the hearers."* The corrupt words that proceed from the heart through evil thoughts defile a man. They also create doorways for the tempter.

The Narrow Way And Our Dressing Mode

The narrow way is to dress appropriately and decently. It is to keep under cover the sensitive parts of the body, (the breasts, buttocks, thighs, stomach etc.) so that they do not cause a distraction that will lead innocent souls to temptation and sin; and the punishment that sin attracts. The Word of God makes us to understand that we are responsible for the well-being of our fellow human beings and should not allow our habits or what we perceive as freedom to negatively influence them and to drag them to the condemnation of God. This means that we should set good examples not bad ones (Rom.14:13b).

Everybody has a final appointment with God Who

created all in His own image. He has specified the appropriate outfit any who will appear before Him for judgement should always put on in the world. The book of Rom. 13:14 states; *"But put ye on the Lord Jesus Christ, and make not provision for the flesh, to fulfil the lust in it."* You should wear the characteristics and attributes of Jesus which is also that of God, as a garment. On the physical, you should dress in the way the Bible specified as appropriate. This has been dealt with in the section on the .spirit of the last days. Those who do not wear what is appropriate for their gender go against the Biblical injunctions on dressing.

Man is supposed to be grateful to God for whatever gender He made them to be. An indecent and provocative manner of dressing lures people to sin. A child of this age says that most outfits are unisex. Another supports this by saying that clothing has no gender. Times may have changed but the Word of God does not and abides for ever. God is still the Ancient of Days, and His Words are Ye and Amen to His Glory through us.

The Light of Christ as the Narrow Way

The light of the gospel reveals the teachings, ministry, and life of Christ. Through this light, man has to live in order to enlighten his areas of darkness. Jesus is the Light of man. The Word of God in 1 Cor.13:12 says that man sees as in a glass darkly. The Bible says that the Light of Christ cannot be withheld by any darkness in the world (Jn.1:4-5). Once Light appears, darkness flees automatically.

In Jn. 12:46 Jesus said; "*I am come as Light to the world, that whosoever believeth in me shall not abide in darkness.*" He repeated this fact in Jn. 8:12 by saying that whoever believes and lives in Him will have the light of life, which means the right way to live in this world of darkness that will not attract the wrath and the condemnation of God in the end. Without Christ's Light, the pitfalls in the life of man, may prove insurmountable.

Man may be empowered to perceive truly beyond the physical, but cannot by themselves combat the physical and spiritual dangers in life. The way has to be cleared and enlightened by the Light of the gospel which is Christ. Only Jesus can baptise with the Holy Spirit which believers so desperately need in order to have the Light and be able to abide in the Shadow of the Almighty.

Without Jesus there will be no eternal life for according

to Rom. 8 :2 it is the life in Him that separates man from sin and eternal death. Without Him man cannot have newness of life through His Light. 2 Cor.5:17.

The Food We Eat

Rom. 14:15-16 reads: *"Yet if your brother is grieved because of your food, you are no longer walking in love. Do not destroy with your food the one for whom Christ died. Therefore do not let your good be spoken of as evil."* This fact emphasises the need to exercise restraint in the practise of liberty. If you do to your neighbour only that which you will that he will do to you, you will not lead them into temptation.

The scriptures in Mk. 7:19 and 1 Tim.4:3-5 requires that food and drink be sanctified by thanksgiving and prayers before it is taken.. Some food are defiled, in the process of preparation, some unhealthy or even dangerous, spiritually or physically. Some produce excess sugar, salt or fat in the body. The Word of God says that the Kingdom of God is not meat and drink but peace, righteousness and joy in the Holy Spirit (Rom.14:17).

Conclusion

This chapter ends with emphasis on the fact that without the inclination to follow in obedience, one may as well forget the narrow way. The demons believe also in God and tremble. Js. 2:19. In the Bible they acknowledge Christ as the Son of God Matt. 8:29, although they neither obey God nor Christ. Likewise any believer who is aware of the requirements of the Narrow way but does not necessarily strive to follow it will remain on the wide way. Man's problem is primarily that of disobedience to His Creator. At no time in the history of man is this obedience more necessary than at this perilous times, for many reasons.

The restless signs in the environment confirming the original prophecies by Christ Himself, that the end is near (Matt. 24:7-14, 2 Tim.3:1-5, Rev.13 1-10; The spiritual indicators confirming the same message; the turning of the Word of God upside down; the dire consequences of sin (Ez. 18:4b; Rom. 6:23 Heb. 10:26); The impending judgement of God on man and the commencement of the process to terminate the present heaven and earth.

These are perilous times of violence and conflicts, when many are being initiated in ignorance while some are perishing spiritually. Obedience as a result of repentance can unlock the key of mercy from God.

The advice I was given by a spiritual visitor was this. "Whatever He asks you to do, do it." This is a simple meaningful injunction to obey, and was the same answer spoken to the messengers by Mary the mother of Christ at the marriage in Cana. (Jn 2:5).

In Lk. 24:44, after the resurrection, Jesus spoke the following Words to His disciples. *These are the Words which I spoke to you while I was yet with you that all things must be fulfilled which were written in the Law of Moses, and in the prophets, and in the psalms concerning me.*" Today, Christ is saying to us, Children, so shall all the requirements in the scriptures pertaining to salvation and the need to walk on the Narrow way be required of you through obedience to the Word and the Holy Spirit. It is irrelevant whether the fulfilment will be interesting, shameful or agonising; for the end will justify the means by faith. Obedience is the only way to the righteousness of Christ.

.

Every day millions and millions of requests are tabled to God through Christ by those seeking for healing, deliverance, provision and peace, from all the many ills and afflictions of man. What answer would a believer imagine that God would always give to all these increasing number of requests? He may ask the following questions. Children can we say that disobedience to my Word is a major reason for all these problems? Do we read the Word every day and meditate on it sufficiently in order to obey it?

Isa. 26:3 states, *"Thou wilt keep Him in perfect peace, whose mind is stayed on thee, because he trusteth in thee."* Stayed here means to read, meditate and act on what one reads. It is necessary that one prays every day for the will and strength to obey the Word. If we can remember that we are under strict surveillance and that anytime we sin, Jesus is upset with us, we may be more careful with and obedient to the Word.

THE DEGENERATED MORAL VALUES

Morality is at its lowest ebb at this end time, and there seems to be an unconscious conspiracy of silence about its continuous degeneracy. The old moral values based on the Word of God, are cast aside to make way for loose innovative practices that expose and encourage the abuse of liberty. Shameless examples are set for the young, which they pick up very fast. How far this trend will continue is yet unknown. Maybe until the return of Christ.

No man has been proved sinless. Man can only attain partial sinlessness through the grace of God. How then can a sinful man's acquired knowledge be compared to, or be perceived to be superior to that of God Who is completely sinless and teaches knowledge to all? (Ps. 94:10) How can man who left on his own, cannot save himself be able to save another? The danger in substituting God's wisdom with that of human, is that the person being saved will end up taking on the sins, shortcomings and weaknesses of the one claiming to save them.

The right moral conduct based on the Word of God, centre on righteousness, love, faith in God, peace, purity of heart, humility gentleness, discipline, forgiveness etc. Changes brought about by technology, philosophy, the spirits of the antichrist, social customs, tradition, the flesh, man's quest for pleasure and ease, have eroded these sound moral principles. These changes are responsible for the carnal spirits of idolatry, adultery and fornication, strife, hatred, anger covetousness, pride, selfishness, violence, wars and killings that are very prevalent in the lives of most people of this age. The Shadow of the Almighty is very far removed from these.

Scriptural Guidelines Against Moral Laxity

The neglect of these principles will not allow one to get to the Shadow of the Almighty. For most, it may be a reminder of what they are already aware of, but tend to neglect.

1. Lawlessness is the mother of moral decadence. Jesus said in Matt. 5:17 *"Think not that I am come to destroy the Law, or the prophets; I am not come to destroy but to fulfil."* Christ is the beginning and end of all righteousness.

2. 1 Cor. 3:17 says: *"If any man defiles the temple of God, him shall God destroy; for the temple of God is holy, which temple ye are."* Holiness is the foundation on which good morals thrive. How many of us are truly determined to obey Christ and live holy? Most of us are determined, but still struggling to obey. The Holy Spirit will make this possible for us in Jesus Name. The Word of God says that we shall present our bodies as instruments of righteousness to God (Rom.6:13).

3. Matt. 12:35-36 says, *"A good man out of the good treasure of the heart bringeth forth good things and an evil man out of the evil treasure bringeth forth evil things."* There is a great need for man to control the thoughts of his heart from which all defilement flows. This is a very challenging exercise that all are required to take seriously.

4. Gal. 5:16 reads: *"This I say then, walk in the Spirit and you shall not fulfil the lust of the flesh."* The flesh in man lusts for the enticements in the world and this gives rise

to sin. The flesh is continually under this temptation. This is where self-control as a fruit of the spirit comes in. It is the distractions, enticements in the world that stir up the satanic demands in the flesh of man, which without the help and power of the Holy Spirit, no one can withstand. This is the reason for the degenerate state of moral decadence in the world today. The tendency for man to be subject to the world and not to the Word.

In John 16:33 Jesus has a solution. He says; *"... be of good cheer, for I have overcome the world."* It is faith in Christ that can overcome the world. When man follows Jesus in faith, and walks according to the Spirit, he can be able to overcome the temptations of this world.

5. 1 Tim. 5:1, *"Rebuke not an elder, but entreat him as a father; and the younger men as brethren; the elder women as mothers; the younger as sisters, with all purity."* Most people in this generation have lost touch of this principle of showing respect to the elderly generation including their parents. Loving God with all our mind soul and strength, conditions one to love and respect others.

6. 1 Tim. 6:17-18, *"Charge them that are rich in this world,*

that they be not high-minded, nor trust in uncertain riches, but in the living God, Who giveth us richly all things to enjoy; That they do good, that they be rich in good works, ready to distribute, willing to communicate." It is God Who according to Deut. 8:18 gives one the power to make money, and according to Isa. 48:17 gives the power to make profit, so that he may be able to share with those who do not have (2 Cor.9:8) and to fulfil ones obligations in the Church. Do not allow riches to corrupt you but use it to glorify God.

It can be seen that the principles of good moral behaviour is rooted in the Bible, which is the Will of God for man. Moral standard of behaviour is based on the practice of scriptural principles of the Bible. If anyone looses sight of what the Bible is saying, especially at this perilous times, the person may likely find themselves afloat in a sinking world of confused ideas. We shall use the following illustration to show the extent of moral imperfection that can penetrate the life of a born again Christian, who allows the interest of the world to rule his life.

An Illustration Demonstrating Moral Imperfection

Let us say that this particular Christian has been born

again for some years now. He is not a regular Bible reader, but prefers to spend most of his time on the internet programmes. He makes it clear that he does not want any unnecessary burden to be placed on him because he is a born again Christian. He strongly questions the scripture in Acts 14:22 which states that, *"Through temptation and tribulation we shall enter the Kingdom of heaven".* He is clever, interesting and fun loving, to an extent. He is always happy and resents anything that will challenge this easy relaxed way of life he has chosen. He strongly believes that this happiness is part of the joy of the Holy Spirit in Gal. 5:22 and as a result is always confessing that the joy of the Holy Spirit is his strength.

He also misunderstood the scriptures because the joy of the Holy Spirit is the promised joy of the kingdom in the end as a result of obedience to the Word of God. We focus on the end like Jesus in Heb. 12:2, *"Who for the joy that was set before Him ignored the cross and despised the shame, and is now sitting down at the right hand of the throne of God."* Like some end time youths, he is very self-centred and has not made a habit of sacrificing his interests for that of God. He does not believe that temptations, trials and suffering are part of being prepared for salvation and that he can grow in endurance, self-control, diligence etc.

When his friend reminded him that the Church as announced, should be starting their fast the following day, he confessed that he forgot all about it, but would see how many days he could manage. He was more concerned about missing his appointment with his girlfriend at the cinema the following day. He however assured his friend that he would still keep his appointment but will not buy anything to eat or drink as usual. He claimed that all these rules are however mere religious appendages, because salvation is a matter of the heart. He forgot that it is from the heart that the thought of lusting for a girlfriend, going out with her on a fasting day instead of staying in the house to fast and pray originated too. Actually he did not eventually participate in the fasting programme.

He is unconsciously compromising the Word of God in order to promote his own standard of world behaviour. His favourite Bible passage is Rom.10:9, "...*if you will confess with your mouth the Lord Jesus Christ, and believe in your heart that God raised Him from the dead, you shall be saved.*" His understanding of this scripture did not go beyond its literal translation. He did not understand the fact that belief in Jesus should be reflected in the way one thinks, speaks and acts. Action is a manifestation of what is thought or believed.

"Hello brother, you are quite early for this programme again." says his friend to him. "Yes; just to make sure that I secure a sit at the front row, as it is usually a crowded programme." He comes early because of his own convenience not to obey the rule of being punctual.

When the speaker entered, he was the first person to jump up and began to clap. He also seemed to be responding well to the programme from all appearances. However it was observed that during the discussion session he had no contribution to make. His mind was elsewhere in the world all that time he was pretending to be listening to the programme. When his view was later sought by his friends, he replied that silence is not indicative of ignorance, and that he was okay. What the speaker was saying fell on the way side of his mind and Satan carried them away Matt.13:3-4.

His friend quickly retorted; "But you are always complaining that you do not speak in tongues and are not receiving from God. Don't you think that absent mindedness may be one of the reasons for these?

The scriptural lessons from this illustration are as follows. Though he was born again he has not allowed the Spirit to operate in him. . He is a carnal Christian, yet to be born again in the Spirit. 1 Cor.3:1-2. Friendship with the world is enmity with God. He is not changing because his decisions are still selfishly motivated 2 Cor. 5:17.

A selfishly motivated person cannot accept the Truth because it is contradictory to his interests. He needs to read, study and understand the word more. His unbelieving friends unfortunately do not seem to be learning much from him. He needs to come to a good knowledge of the promises of God for him in the Bible so that he can be encouraged. He needs love and encouragement rather than discouraging criticisms. He may change and become better than many other believers Heb.10:23. He does not want to carry his cross and that inability to endure his cross, and trust in Jesus alone, will hinder his spiritual growth. Matt. 10:38.

In Matt 16:24 Jesus said that those who want to follow Him should deny themselves, take up their cross and come. In Matt. 10:38 He said, *"And he that taketh not his cross and followeth after me is not worthy of me."*

143

What Is This Cross?

It was that Cross that bore and endured man's punishment for sin. The Cross makes you to acquire part of Christ's nature, as you willingly come to terms with the shame, suffering and afflictions that are part of Christian life. Some who do not necessarily want to be associated with this teaching, believe that since salvation is by grace, Christ has endured all the suffering for them at the Cross. They forget that it is only through identifying with this Cross that one can attain the grace of Salvation.

1. The cross can arise as a result of the pain of denying the satanic demands of the flesh Gal.5:24.

2. It can come as a result of the open doorways which disobedience to the Word can give rise to Eccl.10:8.

3. It is the cross of suffering that can arise as a result of the fulfilment of the Great Commission of Matt. 28 18-19

4. It can be a cross of affliction imposed and reinforced by the evil foundation of your father's or mother's house which is laid on that of Satan. 1 Cor.3:11.

5. It can be a cross of suffering and shame which the evil one himself can install and reinforce as a result of one being unequally yoked with unbelievers. 2 Cor.6:14-18.

6. It can be imposed by the enemy whenever he foresees a great blessing of God about to come into the life of

believers Jn. 10:10.

7. It can be the cross brought upon you by an unrepentant enemy within the family whom you may even be praying for Matt. 10:36.

8. It can be due to the fact that there exist a good relationship between you and Christ 2 Cor. 5:17.

Abiding in the Shadow of the Lord does not mean that all problems are over. This world is filled with problems and until you get to heaven you can only have some periods of relief, strengthening and training. The purpose of these is to encourage persistence in righteousness. How many people are getting on with their walk and do not mind the burden of their cross because they believe that Christ is perfectly able to lift them off their shoulders at an appropriate time? 1 Pet. 5:10 says; *"...after you have suffered, He will perfect, establish, strengthen and settle you."*

How many feel that they will not be able to continue with their burden, and as a result are moaning and complaining about it although they know that Christ has the power to get rid of it for them? We have come to understand that the habits of long suffering and endurance come as a result of affliction and suffering.

How many have decided that the alternative of drifting along with the world in its enticements, lusts and satanic pleasures is more preferable than a whole life of endurance and goodness? Gal. 6:7 reads; *"Do not be deceived. God is not mocked, for whatsoever a man sows that he will reap."* Apart from idolatry and pride, one may dare to presume that another sin that stinks in the eyes of God may be that of immorality. Reasons why this sin is considered very serious are obvious. It is committed against the body and our bodies are regarded as the temples of the Holy Spirit. Other sins are outside the body. 1 Cor. 6:18-20 reads: *"Flee fornication. Every sin that a man doeth is outside the body; but he that commiteth fornication sinneth against his own body. What? Know ye not that your body is the temple of the Holy Ghost which is in you, which ye have of God, and ye are not your own? For ye are bought with a price; therefore glorify God in your body, and in your spirit, which are God's."*

Jesus is man's example of correct moral standing. We need to follow Him. Jesus has no moral lust for the world and cannot be swayed by it. He is the way out of the unprecedented moral decadence of this present era.

Today, the evil one himself, is set to turn every biblically established moral standard upside down, because many are still not interested in getting to know the Word that leads to Christ and Salvation.

These times are considered perilous, in human history. It is the age of moral debasement and negative permissiveness. According to the divine visitation I had, I was asked how like Jesus I have become, and told that judgement will be based on this fact.

THE SHADOW OF THE ALMIGHTY FOR THE EXTREMELY DEPRESSED

To the extremely depressed, and as a result prone to suicidal tendencies, abiding in the shadow of the Almighty should be sought with aggressive determination. This is because when you are vulnerable, and unable to control the movement of your thoughts, anything your thoughts alight on, Satan will immediately work through it to lead you further to contemplate what is sinful and sometimes unimaginable. This situation can degenerate into the unexpected if left to continue. The need then arises for one always to exercise due control over his mind at all times, especially for anyone aspiring to abide in the Shadow of the Almighty. Most importantly is the need to exercise one's faith in the ability of God through the Holy Spirit to focus the mind only on what is right.

Extreme Case of Depression

Extreme depression is a state of mind in which a strange satanic domineering and controlling spirit takes control of the mind, and directs its thoughts and actions. It is more prevalent in the young than in the old. This can be as a result of the new ideas based on technology, the new age movement, social media, the need to explore the unknown that is prevalent in this age. This is a desperate state of mind in which one is made to believe that all hope even in God is lost, and the only thing left is how to terminate life.

The Word of God has made us to understand that our bodies belong to Him Who created us in His own image, and that Jesus has paid a ransom with his blood for everybody. The destruction of that body becomes a sin before God. Ex. 20:13. Every life is precious in the eyes of God, Who has set a purpose on earth for it. The day a life comes into the world is usually a day of great joy for the parents, relatives and friends. This same life is not supposed to be terminated in shame.

The feeling of extreme anxiety is a stronghold set up in the mind by the spirit of uncertainty and fear. This spirit sooner or later becomes a lying idol in the mind and begins to destroy one's confidence and faith in the ability of God to deliver and save.

Factors Responsible

Some factors responsible for depressive cases are as follows: Family breakdown or parental neglect, abuse or violence; examination pressure, bad company and environment, hereditary factors, online films, racism, lack of faith in God and His Word, the wrong concept of evolution, wrong perception of self, sharp financial decline. Some hear voices that mislead them into harming themselves. Unfortunately the religious studies taught in the schools to nurture the mind and maintain right moral standards have been severely slashed and compromised.

The scriptural evidence of Christ's miraculous works are termed old fashioned, no longer interesting enough. In the book of Prov. 14:12, it is written that there is a way that seems right to many, but the end of that way is destruction. Jn. 17:17 states that the Word of God is the Truth, and John. 8:32 states that you shall know this Truth, and it shall set you free.

Things That We Need To Be Reminded Of About God

God loves everybody especially the youths. They occupy a special place in His heart; maybe because they are a relevant part of His end-time ministry. He understands all their problems because like some of them, he also suffered rejection (Matt. 9:4), conspiracy (Matt. 26:4), workload pressure (Jn. 5:17; Jn 4:34), lack of accommodation (Luke 9:58). He may not approve of the way some are trying to find solutions to these problems, and will like them to resort to the scriptures which has solutions to all the problems that man can ever experience. The unbelieving Scribes and Pharisees refused to listen to what He was saying but continuously plotted to take away His Life Jn. 1:11. Accommodation was a big problem. He was wandering about in the desert without shelter.

All He is saying is that people should first repent of all the sins that came into their lives as a result of these problems, then come in faith to Him so that the sins can be forgiven and everything put right. Their unrighteousness He will forgive, and their misdeeds He will remember no more.

He will cleanse their blood that He has not cleansed, seeing that some did it in ignorance and unbelief. His love for them is stronger than all the sins they committed; and with their faith in the power of Christ's death and resurrection to save them, He can lead them to a new life. Paul the apostle said in 1 Tim. 1:13, *"I was a blasphemer, a persecutor, and an idolater, but the Lord forgave me because I did it in ignorance and unbelief."*

Are you worried that your sins are too bad to be presented to God? Forget it. The love of God for you, is stronger than that sin Jn. 15:13; and Christ's shed blood washes whiter than snow Ps. 51:7. Are you one of those who believe that you have no more hope and faith in the ability of anyone to help you, even God inclusive? You are indirectly undermining the power and love of God for you, which is stronger and more reliable than any power and love you may be searching for. You are indirectly condemning yourself to eternal damnation in hell. In Jn. 16:33, Jesus said; *"These things I have spoken to you, that in me you may have peace. In the world you will have tribulation; but be of good cheer. I have overcome the world."*

The Role of the Church

The power to reject the spirit of extreme depression and suicide, comes from God through accepting His Son Jesus Christ and the Holy Spirit. Before His death and resurrection, Christ deposited some of His powers in the Church which is His Body. The Church is supposed to operate in the power of the Holy Spirit through prayers and deliverance to perform those miracles which Christ performed while He lived on this earth (Jn. 14:12-14). This is why the Church has a a big responsibility in dealing with this problem of extreme depression. The root cause of this mental health problem is attributed to worry and anxiety. This is why the Words of Jesus in the book of Lk. 12:22-23 says, *"Therefore I say to you, do not worry about your life, what you will eat, nor about the body, what you will put on. Life is more than food, and the body is more than clothing."*

Worrying or anxiety, cannot provide any needed help because God Who created all the organs of man and monitors the workings of the heart has the power to minister divine healing. Anxiety is considered sinful because it denotes a lack of faith in the ability of God to heal. The political agenda for the Church which was handed over to her by Christ can be seen in the book of Isa. 61: 1-3. The first verse reads;

"The Spirit of the Lord is upon Me,
Because He has anointed Me
To preach good tidings to the poor;
He has sent Me to heal the broken hearted,
To proclaim liberty to the captives,
And the opening of the prison to those who are bound;"

This mandate incorporates the need to be set free from the bondage of extreme depression and suicide. Ps. 107:20 reads, *"He sent His Word and healed them, and delivered them from their destructions."* Through deliverance prayers and the understanding and application of the Word, many people have been delivered from this bondage.

Churches Must Work Hard to Fulfil these Needs:

1. It is the responsibility of the Church to make sure that children are well grounded in the scriptures so that as they grow they will learn to avoid the end time problems of growing up.

2. Some Churches have set up different child fellowship groups, camp activities and effective counselling sessions for the young and are effectively reaching out to the

children and youths.

3. The Church can also play an advisory role to the state if allowed, by giving the state the right guidance as laid down by Christ in its doctrines.

4. The Church can make sure that people come to terms with the important biblical principles of life, since an absence of this can lead to the inability to deal with problems like rejection, anxiety and its eventual outcome. This also may lead to God's condemnation at the end of the age (Heb.1 0:26).

Although genuine Christians also feel alienated, that they are not really part of this world because of the persecutions and attacks (human and spiritual) which they encounter they are not driven to suicide or self-harm but closer to Jesus.

5. The Church counsels individuals and seeks the face of God for knowledge on how to conduct deliverance prayers for the extremely depressed. She is also able to advice according to scriptural requirements.

6. The Church can pass them through deliverance and after deliverance sessions. These may include prayers and counselling for their parents, relatives. The patients or clients can be introduced to those who have passed through similar problems and were fully delivered. This

gives encouragement and builds up faith.

God has to forgive first, before he can release the anointing that will take care of the evil spirit. This is where repentance and confession of sins come in. We all were born in sin Ps. 51:5. Some of us had the privilege of reading and listening to the Word of God; thought deeply about it, repented and humbly came before God in prayers pleading for forgiveness Isa.1:18. We were baptised and received the power of the Holy Spirit to help remit those sins. We are now part of the body of Christ studying His Word, and still passing through a process of sanctification by the Holy Spirit.

Why the Thought of Suicide Should Be Avoided

Thought of committing suicide must be avoided because of its dire Consequences, some of which are as follows:
1. Ex. 20:13 says, *"Thou shall not kill."* You shall not take your own life or that of another. God, Whose judgement you will meet immediately you commit suicide gave that mandate. Ez. 18:4b says, *"Behold all souls are Mine; the soul of the father, as well as the soul of the son is Mine The soul who sins shall die."* You have no right to severe the soul that belongs to God from its body.

Terminating your life consciously, is a major sin in the eyes of God, and attracts Gods immediate condemnation and punishment.

Heb. 9:27 states that it is appointed unto man to die once; after death judgement. One needs to prepare carefully for God's judgement than rush into it unprepared Rom. 6:23. There is no punishment on earth that is worse than spending the rest of one's life inside a fire that burns and never quenches. It is also not advisable to hasten one's sojourn there consciously or unconsciously. Jesus said in Matt. 10:28, *"Fear not he who can kill the body; but fear Him Who can cast both body and soul into hell fire."* Only God has the power to do this.

Any victim of suicide has suddenly terminated his or her chances of accepting Jesus as Lord and Saviour, and the subsequent preparation for the heavenly home. If you believe that you have no hope in this world except to harm yourself or take your life, it means that you have not explored all the options open to you. You greatly undermine the love of God for you and are also completely unaware of the destination of the journey that you are about to undertake. You are indirectly calling God a liar in the sense that His son's death and resurrection cannot set you free. You lack faith in the power of the Holy Spirit to lead you successfully away from sin, to Heaven. It is not easy to receive healing or deliverance from God without faith in Jesus. That faith comes through reading and listening to the Word of God.

Say this prayer:
> *I thank You Holy Father God, for explaining to me, the dire consequences of suicide, and saving me from an everlasting punishment of spending eternal life in a burning fire. Please forgive me for trying to destroy a life which Jesus died to save. I repent of all my sins, and accept Jesus as Lord and Saviour. Please lead me on the path of deliverance and salvation in Jesus Name.*

For the prayers needed to get God to deliver from the spirit of suicide you may have to get a copy of the book Pray The Word by the same author.

A major reason for suicide may be attributed to the wrong belief in the evolution of man; that God did not create man after all. This view, in direct opposition to the Word, means the renunciation of allegiance to God the Creator and Maker. The following scriptures seriously contradict this.

Gen. 1:27-28 says: *"So God created man in His Own image. In the Image of God He created him; male and female, He created them. Then God blessed them and said to them; be fruitful and multiply."* Man is walking about in the image of God because of His Love and humility.

Ps. 24:1 reads: *"The earth is the Lord's and the fullness thereof; the world and all who dwell there in. For He has founded it upon the seas and established it upon the rivers."*

All Creation is His Handiwork

Ps. 127:3 reads; *"Lo, children are an heritage of the Lord; and the fruit of the womb is His reward."* He directs the formation of the child in the womb. In Jer. 1:5 God said to Jeremiah; *"Before I formed thee in the belly I knew thee: and before you came out of the womb I sanctified thee, and I ordained thee a prophet unto the nations."*

If man evolved, why is he not doing the same today? Why does a woman have to become pregnant, and have children according to the Word of God in Gen. 3:16? It reads: *"I will greatly multiply your sorrow and your conception. In sorrow you shall bring forth children."*

He who spoke the Heaven and earth into existence and created life, spoke these Words and they are still happening today like all His Words.

CHURCH IN HIS SHADOW

Any Church founded on Christ the Rock has an angel overseeing it and is supposed to be under the Shadow of the Almighty. The purpose is to make the Church spotless for a life in heaven. Every believer must die with Christ at baptism and be raised by faith with Him at His resurrection. This establishes the fact that the foundation of the Church is laid on the blood of Jesus. All believers in Christ must undertake the Abrahamic journey as stated in Heb.11:10 in order to belong to this foundation whose builder is Christ. It reads: *"For he looked for a city which hath a foundation, whose Builder and Maker is God."* This foundation which is based on the Life, Teachings, and Ministry of Christ which He received from God, guarantees the Church a place in His Shadow and in Heaven afterwards.

The seven Churches in Asia Minor can be seen as representing all the Churches at the time of writing the Bible, and also at this present age. They mirror Christ's expectations of Churches that will abide under His Shadow and the ones that will not. Rev.2, 3. The criticisms, corrections and exhortations He issued to them, are also applicable to present day Churches. This is because innate human nature and needs will remain the same, unless the Word of God is allowed to penetrate the heart to effect a change. The only difference is in the way that humans of today satisfy these needs. Education, communication network, technology, philosophy, economic improvements, etc, rather than fulfil these needs, have created new problems which fortunately the same Bible still provides answers for.

The Churches can abide in His Shadow only if in their minds and actions they are following Christ's Ministry on which its doctrines are based. He handed these over to them with the authority to operate in the power of the Holy Spirit. These doctrines centre on winning souls for Christ, care for the needy, healing of the sick, justice for the oppressed, knowledge of God for the hungry or ignorant, freedom for those in bondage, shelter for the homeless and love for God and for all.

These instructions are closely related to the ones that Christ gave to His disciples when He sent them out to win souls in Matt.10:5-25. They are regarded as the guide lines which the Churches should follow. They should preach the kingdom message, cast out devils, heal the sick, carry only what is necessary in terms of clothing and materials, not ask for money; minister in faith, humility and love and expect persecution, attacks and martyrdom if possible. When they encountered any problems they should expect the help of God. There is a difference in the scope of the two assignments. Whereas then they were required to preach only to the Jews, after the resurrection He specifically commissioned that the gospel should be taken to the whole world.

These instructions which are based on His doctrines for the Church are supposed to act as a uniting belt that will make them attain the type of unity which Paul emphasized in 1Cor 1:10 and abide in His Shadow. When Paul also spoke to the Philippians in Phil.2:2, he emphasised the need to operate in one mind, love, judgement, and faith. He was committed to spiritual unity. Genuine unity comes from having the same belief, mind and purpose. Some who claim to support unity, do not believe that hell fire exists but purgatory, and some that there is no resurrection, others that Jesus is not the Son of God, while some that you do not have to strive in order to enter heaven because once saved always saved, and many according to 1 Jn.2:18, are giving heed to deceiving spirits and doctrines of demons, etc. Any such unity is of the world and not of the Spirit.

These are serious underlying fundamental differences that only the Holy Spirit who operates in the mind can sort out. Pro. 21:1. How can you have the Holy Spirit and the power to give up sin, (Acts.1:8) without having Jesus? He is the only one Who can baptise you with the Holy Spirit Matt. 3:11b. How can you have Jesus without believing that He is the Son of God (Mk. 9:7b)? How can you believe that He is the Son of God without having faith in Him? How can you develop faith in Christ without hearing and reading the Word of God? Rom.10:17.

The Holy Spirit came to unite the minds of believers in Christ in all the Churches. It is only through Him that one can access God or attain salvation. This serious matter does not give any room for compromise. Divisiveness of the mind and fake unity has no place in the Shadow of the Almighty. True unity is a very vital requirement for all believers because it transcends from the Triune God to the Church, and to the family.

While under the Shadow of the Almighty, the Church while in the world, still faces challenges, but these are overcome by the Holy Spirit. An example is the Church in Philadelphia who overcame through persevering in faith and obeying the Word of God Rev.3: 10 -11. Within some Churches and across some others, there are contentions. The true unity of believers is by faith in Christ Jesus, obedience to the Holy Spirit and the Word. The Church's credibility is established by a good knowledge of Christ through the Word. If any Church decides to work contrary to Christ's doctrines, thereby challenging His authority and hindering His Glory, He has the power to discipline that Church. He can put off its light.

In the book of Rev.2 and 3, the critical observations brought against five of the seven Churches included having a love for God that lacks fervency. Other observations are heresy, tolerance of immorality, idolatry, a weak faith, and indifference. He was very specific on the particular disciplinary action that He would take against any Church that was compromising the Word. In 1Cor.5:1-2, 11, Paul criticised the Corinthians for tolerating the spirit of immorality in their midst.

Contrary doctrines like the lack of love for one another, different goals, unholy competitions, strife, criticisms, selfish ambitions, love of money and sectionalism, largely contribute to the disunity of the Church. These shortcomings, create difficulty in continuing to abide in the Shadow of God.

The Word of God does not compromise its meaning in order to meet with the changing times. It had been programmed to take care of all the changes of the entire age. If a Church decides that because of societal quest for financial growth it now has to concentrate a greater part of its preaching on prosperity, to the neglect of spiritual topics like holiness and righteousness, salvation, restitution, restoration and all such teachings, this will definitely result in a downward slope in its spiritual growth. This will adversely affect the number of people who will make heaven from there.

Some type of believers spend a considerable length of their time searching for the churches that will satisfy their immediate needs. The financially disabled says; "I will go to that Church because they preach financial prosperity." The one labouring under foundational bondage says: "I will go to this one because they have a strong deliverance Ministry." The one set on marriage says: "Hardly any youth gets married in my Church. I have to make a change." The one looking for the fruit of the womb says, "I have heard that most of those who go to that Church are immediately blessed with children." Another says, "Too many people are dying in this Church; I have to move away with my family before it is too late". Sometimes this roving inclination is never satisfied and becomes a habit. Although one cannot be blamed for seeking the most available Christian solution to their problems, this perception which is manmade, may mislead new converts coming to the body of Christ and eventually affect their faith. They may not be able to perceive each Church as a composite of the fullness of Christ.

With adequate faith, the power in one Church can also be experienced in another irrespective of size and number. This is what Paul referred to as an abuse of the Christian law of liberty. One should be sensitive to the comments they make about Churches and the effect on the young in Christ or unbelievers so that they do not lead them to stumble. Rom 14:13.

All the powers were bestowed on all the Churches by Jesus through the Holy Spirit. The Holy Spirit blessed the Churches with different spiritual gifts and fruits, to be used for its edification.1 Cor.12:4-11. As they operate in faith and obedience, the necessary anointing to get these problems sorted out are released. I had a revelation of a Church that was not full that suddenly was filled up. Then I heard a voice that said "Wrong people." The size of a Church does not necessarily determine entry into the Kingdom. The one that is contemplating a move may be one of those that God planned to use to manifest His power in that particular Church. That movement may prove to be a spiritual disaster.

The Holy Spirit was sent to unite the Body of Christ in Him, so that they will walk with one mind and objective, set for a spiritual growth that will lead to the likeness of Christ.

Eph.4:13 reads: *"Maintain the unity of the Spirit, by walking in the bond of peace."* Eph.4:3-6 talks of one body, spirit, faith, baptism, food. Verses 14 and15 talks of moving towards the measure of the Stature of Christ. Jesus has a Word of encouragement for the end time Churches which are currently facing unusual challenges.

This can be likened to the Word of God to Zerubbabel in Zech.4:6 which reads: *"Not by might nor by power, but by my Spirit, says the Lord of hosts."* Zerubbabel had only laid the foundation of the Temple and being extremely discouraged, was about to give up. Verse 7 says; "Who art thou O great mountain? Before Zerubbabel thou shall become a plain." The Temple which was difficult to build then became easy through the power of the Holy Spirit. It is necessary that end time believers especially those under persecution continue to operate in the power of faith, endurance, and obedience in order to allow God to complete the work He started.

The woman in the book of Rev.12:6 represents the persecuted, witnessing Church that took flight into the Shadow of the Almighty. Here God has made a provision to feed and protect her and she is supposed to endure any suffering patiently. The age long spiritual battle is for all the Churches.

Some Expectations From The Word For Churches Under God's Shadow

Though some Churches are already aware of these expectations the weight of the attack of the evil one, should not be taken for granted. More prayers to strengthen the faith and determination of the body of Christ in order to overcome are needed at this end time. Churches under the Shadow of the Almighty, are supposed to dwell with each other in the unity that exists between the Triune. This also involves thinking speaking and living in Christ. Churches should not criticise or underscore one another, but be willing to extend help and to learn from others. 2 Cor. 9:12.

Jesus the Son of God, acted selflessly by laying aside His glory in order to be slain for our salvation. In like manner, His Body, the Church is expected to forego personal and sectional interests and focus on that of the Church so that its unity remains uncompromised.

The body of Christ is supposed to maintain the fervency of that first love they had when they gave their lives to Christ, and to teach the world how to live in the love of God Rev. 2:4. It is the responsibility of the Church to keep the fire burning. Christ wants a Church that will endure persecution and suffering, joyfully like the Church in Smyrna which He commended. Rev. 2:8-11. This is a Church that will continue to walk in the fear of God. It is faith that makes endurance to thrive.

Christ spoke a lot about the need to maintain continuity in the walk with Him. The Church is expected to continue to strengthen the goodness of God in their lives. Rev. 2:10b. The Church is expected to portray to the world the Christlikeness in them, and to concentrate on winning souls for Him (Jn. 15-16).

The Church is trying to make the world realise that success is to be measured by the knowledge and practice of the Word of God. This leads to the wisdom of God. It should not be by any social or intellectual attainment which is the wisdom of man. Jesus wants His Body to realise and also to make the world realise that true leadership is through servant like humility and forbearance, and not by domination and control as is done in the world (Jn. 13: 13-14).

The Church tries to make people come to the realisation that it is only by the grace of GOD that one can receive true prosperity that will last, which comes through the righteousness of God, and not through sinful acts, Josh. 1:8. Jesus will like the Church to understand that evil can only be defeated through good; and this fact will assume a pattern when we have Jesus rooted in our lives through the Holy Spirit.

It is important that in the Church the fact of Christ's imminent arrival is seriously emphasised including its implications of judgement for the human race; that the only route out of the punishment for sin, is faith in the Lord Jesus and Love for God and fellow humans. Though the Love of God for man is still there, man has to accept and not reject it by walking contrary to His Will. Our God is not responsible for the suffering but the evil one, and sin that comes as a result of human error. We must note that flesh and blood cannot inherit the kingdom of God, but a body born again in the Spirit.

Conclusion

It is the will of God that through His Spirit, obedient believers should dwell in His Shadow. This abode requires a humble, contrite and obedient heart; one that can endure hardship without complaint. The song writer asks; "Do you tread the steep and thorny way rejoicing?" In the Shadow of the Almighty one is supposed to love, serve, bless, save, go out of their way to help, pray for the protection of others, and also for the enemy.

In Ps. 2:1-3 David asks: *"Why do the heathens rage and the people imagine a vain thing? The kings of the earth set themselves, and the rulers take council together against the Lord and against His anointed saying, let us break their bands asunder, and cast away their cords from us."* This prophetic scripture accurately puts in clear perspective what is happening today. The world has gone to great lengths to institute measures to enable man to off load the crosses they are carrying. Man is supposed to endure the effect of these crosses without complaint with faith in the ability of God to lead him away from them. Jesus said in Matt. 16:24: *"If any man will come after me, let him deny himself and take up his cross and follow me."* In Matt. 10:38 He added, *"And he that taketh not his cross and followeth Me, is not worthy of Me."* This is a clear and neat summary of what it takes to abide and grow in His Shadow, and attain Salvation.

He is speaking to every believer and non-believer today, both individually and corporately as His Body, to deny and slay every satanic desire of the flesh, so that they can willingly follow Him with their crosses and learn from Him.

Jesus wants to be glorified in the Church so that it can attract more believers. This should be done through practically living the Kingdom life; a sacrificial spiritual life fit for Christ's disciples. Obedience should be with willingness and love, not by compulsion. Believers are to live according to the law of the Spirit of Life, which is in Christ Jesus. Rom. 8:2; and to flee from the law of sin and death, which is the flesh and the world.

There are many benefits to be derived by dwelling in His Shadow. It is supposed to be a natural home for believers who are prepared by faith, to disregard self and suffering. According to the book of Phil. 4:13 the Power of God can keep one growing in His Shadow from glory to glory. God is happy and glorified as they worship and serve Him in righteousness.

An important factor in abiding in the shadow of the Almighty is that you will be encouraged to bear good fruits. People will notice and will be moved to come to Christ because of this.

Under God's Shadow, you will learn to please others first, before self. This attitude fosters the spirit of genuine unity. Paul the Apostle dealt with this need in the book of Rom. 15:2 which reads: *"Let every one of us please his neighbour for his good to edification. For even Christ pleased not Himself; but as it is written. The reproaches of them that reproached thee, fell on me."* This is all about

174

mutual forbearance and love. It shows one's Christian responsibility to others.

Under His Shadow, He will act as your refuge, shield and fortress. Many years back, when we were newly born again, a man of God said something relevant that many people picked up immediately. He emphasised the need to always let Jesus know through prayers every move you intend to make every day, however insignificant that action may seem to you. He is the one who can foretell the success and failure of all devices of the enemy against all human plans and decisions; and has the power of God at His disposal to deal with any works of darkness. He will also be disposed to alert you of the secret plans of the enemy, and how to avert them (Deut. 29:29). If you are in His Shadow, He will reveal to you any impending evil or good. If you are a Christian that always desires to receive only pleasant news from God all the time, then you may lack the spiritual maturity it takes to abide in His Shadow.

In the Shadow of God, the obedient ones will feel the peace of God that passes all understanding. Ps. 94: says: *"Blessed is the man whom you instruct O Lord, and teach out of your law; that you may give him rest from the days of adversity."*

Ps. 27:4-5 is all about the benefits of dwelling in His Shadow. It reads: *"One thing have I desired of the Lord, that will I seek after; that I may dwell in the house of the Lord all the days of my life; to behold the beauty of the Lord, and to enquire in His Temple. For in the time of trouble, He will hide me in his pavilion. In the secret place of His tabernacle shall he hide me. He shall set me high upon a rock."*

The Spirit of the Lord will be pleased to do all these. When you walk in the Shadow of the Almighty you will enjoy the refreshing that is as a result of the presence of the Holy Spirit of God the Father and the Son. You will begin to understand better the Ways of God.

While in His Shadow you have a chance to be fully restored. The Old Testament is about the arrival of Christ the Restorer Whom God gave the command to restore everlasting life to man. Man needs to be restored from an evil foundation to that of the Lord Jesus Christ which is the only foundation for those who would abide under His Shadow. Here the spiritual death will be replaced by eternal life, sin will be replaced by righteousness, fear by faith, the flesh by the Spirit, pride by humility, strife by peace, hatred by love, ignorance by the knowledge of the Word of God, sickness by health, and darkness by Light. God has His methods of doing things. He is always right with time, and His timing is not that of humans. It is the Holy Spirit Who will guide you into His shadow, and will position and empower you to dwell and grow there if you are willing and obedient. It is the most privileged position that anyone can occupy in this world.

According to Joel 2:25-26, He will restore back to you what the locust, the cankerworm the devouring messengers have stolen from you. In Ps.23:3 He promised to restore your life, and lead you in the path of righteousness; and according to Jer. 30;17, He will restore health to you, and heal you of your wounds as He did to Hezekiah in 2 Kgs. 20:1-11 and also in Jn.10:10 where He states that you will be given a more abundant life than you have ever had before, to mention but a few. Most importantly, in Ps. 118:17, He promises that you shall not die, but live to declare and do His work in the land of the living. These promises inspire hope and continued faith because in the book of 2 Cor. 1:20 it is written: *"For all the promises of God in Him are Yea and in Him Amen unto the Glory of God by us."*

Many promises of God to the Israelites in the Old Testament, were fulfilled in the New. An example can be found in Deut. 18:18. In answer to the request of the Israelites through Moses for a prophet who will be speaking to them, God promised to send them His own prophet who would speak His own Words to them. This promise was fulfilled in Jn. 12:49-50, where Jesus said: *"The Words that I speak to you, are not mine. He who sent me, gave me a command what I should say."* He was sent by God to teach how man should walk under His Shadow and qualify for a place in Heaven.

Restoration From Antichrist Doctrines

The unity of the Holy Spirit is in direct opposition to the activities of the different antichrist spirits in the world that are responsible for the different religious and non-religious backgrounds today. Most believers who are privileged to be in God's Shadow also came from different background of sin. People trace their loyalty from their ancestors and first generation fathers instead of from God their Creator through Christ the Redeemer. The Word clearly states in 1 Cor. 3:11 that; *"On no foundation shall anyone lay except on that laid by the Lord Jesus Christ."* In Col. 2:8 Paul warns the Colossians to be careful *"lest anyone cheat you through philosophy and empty deceit, according to the tradition of men, according to the basic principles of the world and not according to Christ."* You cannot modernise the basic truth of Christianity which is based on satisfying man's need to get away from sin. Whether this need is acknowledged or concealed, it has never changed over the ages since the fall. Everybody needs restoration from one sinful nature or more. Sin is the root of all the problems in the world today. A knowledge of the Word, will make one realise that neither education, technology, modern living, economic advancement, medical inventions, philosophical knowledge, the flesh, etc can provide any solution to the problem of sin in the world. Obedience to the Word of God is more likely to do so.

Abiding in the Shadow of the Almighty may not necessarily create an exemption from the problems and afflictions that the evil one tries to bring on the children of God. It ensures that as you operate in faith and love a divine eye will be watching and commanding those afflictions to go away. David abode in the Shadow of the Almighty, (a man after God's Heart) but he still suffered shame, pain, betrayal and the danger of death, as a result of a sinful mistake. He later confessed that he was happy that he was afflicted so that he could obey the statutes of God. When Jesus lived as a man on this earth, even after forty days of fasting, the devil moved in to tempt him and failed. In His Shadow the assurance of victory is multiplied. Always ask the devil this question: "Do you think that I would agree to be cast into hell? He has the habit of attacking people's faith after every serious fasting program.

Paul walked under the Shadow of God after His conversion, but still suffered excruciating torture, pain and affliction; maybe because Jesus had said that He would show him the great things he would suffer because of Him Acts. 9:16. The Truth about God had already been certified before the coming of Christ Whom He sent so that through Him our faith will be established and firmed up. The sufficiency and power of the Word affirms this. We need to plead with God always to have mercy on us, forgive our weakness and humbly present all our problems before Him. Determination without action lacks the strength and courage needed to abide in His Shadow. The Holy Spirit will bestow His strength and the freedom to overcome. His strength perfects our weakness. 2 Cor. 12:9. Use that power or strength to resist any evil attack through prayers.

SUPPORTING PRAYERS

Aggressive persistent prayers, with faith in the Lord Jesus Christ should be presented before God in righteousness. Prayers that centre on the following needs are particularly advised:

That the Word of God will be made to come alive in the body of Christ more than ever before.

That the body of Christ will receive a divine immunization against all satanic projections in Jesus Name Lk. 1:37.

That God will make a way for the body of Christ where no way seems to be at the moment in Jesus Name. Jn. 14:6.

That God will perfect His plans in the world according to His Word in Jer. 33:15-16.

That the power in the blood of Jesus and the fire of the Holy Spirit be released to challenge any power that wants to mutilate and dehumanise the consciousness of believers in order to render them unfit for the Kingdom in Jesus Name. Rev. 13:16-17.

That the body of Christ should be given a chance to complete their preparation for Heaven without any secret diversion by the enemy in Jesus Name.

That the force of the power of God should render useless the force of the enemy that is attacking the coming of the Kingdom of God (Matt.11:12). in Jesus Name.

In Rev. 9:20-21, the Word of God has made us to understand that even after passing through punishment, some people will still not repent of their sins. When my soul cried out to God about this impending period of darkness that is gradually gathering and the fate of expectant believers at large, I was immediately reminded that there is "absolutely" nothing impossible for God to do.

These prayers reflect a perception of what is going on in the world today. Please do a prayer of thanksgiving and forgiveness before continuing on the following prayers:

1. Rom. 8:2 *"For the law of the Spirit of Life in Christ Jesus has made me free from the law of sin and death."* O Holy God Our Strength and Redeemer, at this dark and perilous time, please enable us through the power of the Holy Spirit, to come closer and closer to your Son Jesus, in Whom is our life; and to go farther away from the flesh, which is of sin and death, in Jesus Name. Eph.4:13.

2. 2 Cor. 12:9 *"My grace is sufficient unto you, for My Strength is made perfect in weakness."* Our Everlasting Father, please empower us always to dwell in Your Grace, and to exercise adequate faith in your power to overcome violent and persistent attacks by spiritual and physical enemies against our lives in the Name of Jesus.

3. 1 Pet. 5:10 *"But the God of all grace, Who has called us to His eternal glory by Christ Jesus, after that ye have suffered a while, make you perfect, establish, strengthen, and settle you."* O Holy Covenant keeping God, please have mercy on us sinners, and do not allow even the weakest among us to shoulder a burden which will prove too heavy for them in Jesus Name.

4. Matt.11:12 *"And from the days of John the Baptist, the*

Kingdom of Heaven suffereth violence, and the violent taketh it by force." The Mighty God of battle, to Whom Alone power belongs, please release the spirit of violent determination and holy aggression in the minds of believers for the spiritual warfare of the Kingdom, in the Name of Jesus.

5. 1 Cor. 2:14 *"But the natural man receiveth not the things of the Spirit of God: for they are foolishness unto him: neither can he know them, because they are spiritually discerned."* O Holy God, The Habitation of Wisdom and Knowledge, please always give us a spiritual perception and understanding of the plans of the enemy against us, so that we do not obey satanic plans in ignorance in Jesus Name. We pray Oh God for a continuous power of discernment in our lives in Jesus Name.

6. Eccl. 8:11 *"Because the sentence against an evil work is not executed speedily, therefore the heart of the sons of man is fully set in them to do evil."* The Eternal Source of all power, Jehovah El-Shaddai, please strengthen our desire and resolve to wait patiently and in obedience for Your Power to avenge for us in Jesus Name.

7. 1 Thess. 5:19 states, *"Do not quench the Spirit."* Rom. 8:10

reads: *"And if Christ be in you the body is dead because of sin, but the Spirit is alive because of righteousness."* Eternal God of all Righteousness, please give us the grace to live in the fruits of the Spirit and not in the flesh; so that we can keep our bodies dead, and the Spirit and it's Fire alive in us, in the Name of Jesus.

8. Hos. 4:6 *"My people are destroyed for lack of knowledge; because you have rejected knowledge I will also reject you."* O Holy God of Right Judgement, as man through his own rejection of the Word has violated your Covenant, please let there be a strong spirit of conviction, repentance, and restoration in the hearts of many in the Name of Jesus.

9. Rev. 13:16 *"And he caused all both strong and great, rich and poor, free and bond to receive a mark in their right hand, or in their foreheads"* O Most Merciful and Righteous Judge, please let the power in the blood of Jesus and the Fire of the Holy Spirit be released to operate against any enemy that is seriously working towards dehumanising your children, by mutilating their consciousness through deceit, in Jesus Name.

10. Rev. 13:17 *"And that no man might buy or sell save he that had the mark, or the name of the beast, or the*

number of his name." O Holy God of Miracles, Signs and Wonders, we pray that the Body of Christ will be given a chance to complete their preparation for Heaven without any spiritual interruptions or diversions, in the Name of Jesus.

11. Isa. 60:1-2 *"Arise, and shine; for the Light is come, and the Glory of the Lord is risen upon thee. For behold the darkness shall cover the earth, and gross darkness the people: but the Lord shall arise upon thee and His Glory shall be seen upon thee."* The Eternal God of Glory, please stir up Your Spirit within us for a more aggressive and persistent prayer life. Let these prayers move your heart to temper judgement with mercy in the lives of Your children in the Name of Jesus. Let Your plans for mankind be finally perfected in Jesus Name.

12. Acts. 2:17-18. *"And it shall come to pass in the last days saith God, I will pour out of my Spirit upon all flesh; and your sons and daughters shall prophesy, and your young men shall see visions, and your old men shall dream dreams. And on my servants and on my handmaidens I will pour out in those days of my Spirit; and they shall* prophesy." O Holy God that keeps Covenant with His people, please help us to get our hearts ready to receive the outpouring

of Your spirit again. Revive us with Your fire and in the Word, so that we shall be able to contend with the attacks and perils of this end time in the Name of Jesus.

13. 2 Pet. 3:10-11, *"But the day of the Lord will come as a thief in the night, in which the Heavens will pass away with a great noise, and the elements will melt with fervent heat; but the earth and the works that are in it will be burned up. Therefore since all these things will be dissolved, what manner of person ought you to be, in holy conduct and godliness?"* Everlasting Creator and Redeemer, since the life of humans on this present earth is fast coming to an end, please empower us to grow more and more in the likeness of Christ; this will guarantee eternal life for believers in the Name of Jesus. Let any plot of the evil one to lead us away from this divine purpose, fail permanently in Jesus Name.

14. Heb. 12:26-27 *"Yet once more I shake not only the earth, but also the Heaven. ...Yet once more indicates the removal of those things that are shaken, as of things that are made, that the things which cannot be shaken may remain."* The Holy God, Whose Judgements are True and Righteous; since the imminent return of Christ will signal the removal of the earthly and temporal things,

please strengthen us and encourage our faith, and empower us to walk on the path of righteousness until He returns, in Jesus Name.

15. Jer. 20:11 *"But the Lord is with me, as a Mighty Awesome One. Therefore my persecutors will stumble, and will not prevail. They will be greatly ashamed for they will not prosper. Their everlasting confusion will never be forgotten."* Oh Thou Awesome and Mighty God, Victorious in battle, please delegate Your warrior angels to bring to utter confusion and failure all the enemies of our souls, in the Name of Jesus.

16. Isa. 51:12 -13, *"I, even I am He Who comforts you. Who are you that you should be afraid of a man who will die? And of the son of man who will be made like grass? And you forget the Lord your Maker, Who stretched out the heavens, And laid the foundations of the earth like a curtain?"* Oh Most Powerful God, Who spoke the heaven and earth into being, please speak permanent fear and failure into the lives of our enemies, in Jesus Name.

17. Rev. 3:10 *"Because you have kept My commandment to persevere, I also will keep you from the hour of trial which shall come upon the whole world, to test those who dwell*

on the earth." Father God of all Mercies and Compassion, please let Your Glorious Right Hand of Power, continue to deliver us from the distresses and tribulations of this end time, in the Name of Jesus.

18. Ez. 21:27 *"I will overturn, overturn, overturn it; and it shall be no more, until He comes Whose right it is and I will give it Him."* Oh God Whose Counsel alone shall prevail, please continue to frustrate the evil devices of Your enemies until Jesus returns to put everything right, in Jesus Name.

19. Jer. 7:8-11, *"Behold, you trust in lying Words that cannot profit. Will you steal, murder, commit adultery, swear falsely, burn incense to Baal, and walk after other gods whom you do not know; and come and stand before Me in this House which is called by My Name? Behold I even I have seen it."* The Holy God Who sees in the secret and in the open, please let Your Kingdom come, and Your Will be finally perfected on this earth even as it is in Heaven. Let the tireless Work of the Holy Spirit for ever glorify You; and may the gates of hell never prevail against Your Church, in Jesus Name.

20. Isa. 66:9 *"Shall I bring to the time of birth, and not cause delivery? says the Lord. Shall I Who cause delivery shut up the womb? says your God."* Most Blessed Holy Spirit of the Living God, please help us to appreciate being part of the Cross, and the reward of endurance, as we pass through the trials and temptations of this age, in Jesus Name.

21. Isa. 27:4 *"Fury is not in me. Who would set the briers and thorns against Me in battle? I would go through them. I would burn them together."* Victorious Warrior, Mighty in battle, please let any power of the enemy, contending with Your Power in our lives, be permanently defeated in the Name of Jesus.

22. 1 Pet. 4:17 *"But the end of everything is at hand; be ye therefore sober, and watch unto prayer"* Everlasting Father please keep us spiritually awake even in our dreams, so that through prayers and Your Power, we can defeat all spiritual fakes in our lives in the Name of Jesus.

23. Ps. 94:20 *"Shall the throne of iniquity, which frameth mischief by law, have fellowship with you? They gather*

themselves together against the soul of the righteous, and condemn the innocent blood." The God that judges in righteousness and truth, please let not the wicked stand in judgement against the righteous in Jesus Name. Empower our desire, determination and strength, to live in increased faith and obedience to your Word, so that You can continue to fight for us and we shall hold our peace, in the Name of Jesus.

24. Ps. 46:10 *"Be still and know that I am God. I will be exalted among the heathen. I will be exalted in the earth."* Holy Father, the Mighty God in battle, we know that Your strength perfects our weaknesses to Your Glory. Please arise, and let all Your enemies be scattered in Jesus Name.

26. Isa. 14:24 *"The Lord of Hosts has sworn saying, Surely as I have thought, so it shall come to pass. As I have purposed it so it shall come to pass."* Thou God, the Habitation of Truth, the established authority of Your Word over the life of man is perfected in Heaven and changes not. Please let Thy Kingdom come, and let Your Will be done on earth in Jesus Name.

27. 2 Cor. :4-5 *"For the weapons of our warfare are not*

carnal, but mighty through God for the pulling down of strongholds, casting down arguments and everything that exalts itself against the Knowledge of God." Everlasting King of glory, please strengthen us to always operate within the limits of the weapons of warfare You gave to us, so that You can eventually fight the battle Yourself for us, in Jesus Name.

28. Deut.33:27 *"The Eternal God is our Refuge and underneath are the everlasting arms, and He shall thrust out the enemy from beneath, and will say destroy."* Eternal Rock of ages, please use our hands as Your battle axe to foil the plan of the enemy to forcibly uproot us from Your body, in Jesus Name.

29. Ex. 20:3 *"Thou shalt have no other Gods before me."* Thou Holy and Mighty God, the Only True God, let any plan of initiation fashioned against Your children in order to divert them to the worship of vain things, whether unconsciously or not, be broken permanently by the power in the blood of Jesus in the Name of Jesus.

30. Isa. 54:15 *"Indeed they shall surely assemble but not because of me. Whosoever assemblies against you, shall fall for your sake."*

Merciful God, please let all the human and spiritual enemies gathered against us, fall for our sakes, in Jesus Name.

31. Isa. 13:9,11 *"Behold the day of the Lord comes, cruel with both wrath and fierce anger. I will punish the world for its evil, and the wicked for their iniquity."* Holy Father God, please in Your wrath, remember Your Body, and also remember mercy; for we all have sinned in different ways, and fallen short of Your glory. Please let Mercy influence judgement in Jesus Name.

The Church is now stepping into the final battle that will qualify her to be the bride of the Lamb. One of the three visions which the Lord gave me about this period in Christian history, depicts a woman in labour, well positioned to push out her child. This time it was a very big white egg that was waiting to come out. This signifies the period of birth pains that the Church is stepping into. Eph.5:27 reads, *"That He might present it to Himself a glorious Church not having spot or wrinkle or any such thing, but that it should be holy, and without blemish."* In Isa. 66:9 God asks, *"Shall I bring to the birth and not cause to bring forth? Said the Lord. Shall I cause to bring forth, and shut the womb?"*

Lightning Source UK Ltd.
Milton Keynes UK
UKHW021009270922
409517UK00006B/88

9 781913 455392